Learning to Teach

A guide for school-based initial
and in-service training

Julian Stern

David Fulton Publishers
London

David Fulton Publishers Ltd
2 Barbon Close, London WC1N 3JX

First published in Great Britain by
David Fulton Publishers 1995

British Library Cataloguing in Publication Data

A catalogue record for this book is available from the British Library

ISBN 1–85346–371–X

Typeset by Harrington & Co
Printed in Great Britain by BPC Books and Journals, Exeter.

Contents

Acknowledgements

South Camden Community School gave me the opportunity to take part in the Institute of Education's school-based teacher training scheme, and both the school and the Institute have supported all the work described in this book. At school, Bob Smith gave me most help as a teacher, along with Betty Hunter (then working for Camden) on language and differentiation; at the Institute, I was particularly helped by Jean Jones. Over the years, many teachers have influenced me, including Nan Grewe (who showed me that teaching could be enjoyable), Barry Dufour (who trained me), Julie Collins (who didn't let me forget how important teaching is), Bill Benge (who showed how helpful managers can be), and Pam Rauchwerger (who corrected this book). Several other schools, many other teachers and support staff, and many many pupils (including those in 11B, my current tutor group at South Camden) deserve credit for making me the teacher I am. It would only be fair for them all to take some of the blame, too.

Marie Stern, of Mortimer School in Lambeth, co-wrote the chapter on bullying. Several sections of the book have been used by Mortimer, who have given their permission to re-use materials; the whole book is influenced by Marie.

I would like to acknowledge the permissions given by Peters Fraser & Dunlop Group Ltd, for Adrian Mitchell's 'Back in the Playground Blues' (taken from *Adrian Mitchell's Greatest Hits – The Top 40;* note that none of Adrian Mitchell's poems are to be used in connection with any examination); Graveney School, for their behaviour policy; The Institute of Education, University of London, for use of materials also published as an OPTET booklet on research (edited by David Lambert and Derek Sankey); and Lesley Bull for the poem 'Bad Box'.

Series Editor's Foreword

This book focuses on three broad concepts: the teacher as researcher, the teacher in the classroom and the teacher outside the classroom. The fifteen chapters are arranged under these three broad headings – together with a fourth, entitled 'Different Perspectives on Education'. This section enables the author to conclude his guide by writing about those key texts which he has found particularly useful – neatly complementing what has gone before.

Obviously, the use of three or four categories in a book of this kind is bound to be somewhat arbitrary, and there is a degree of overlap between the sections. However, the structure of the book does enable the reader to steer a course through the wealth of material on offer. As the sub-title suggests, the book is intended for use by both those students undergoing initial teacher training (particularly where a significant part of that training has a school-based focus), and those teachers who have embarked on some form of in-service training programme as part of their professional development.

Drawing on his own varied experiences in many different sectors of education, Julian Stern provides a personal and stimulating study of what teaching is all about. Theory and practice are viewed throughout as being inter-related, with all school-based research seen as having the common aim of enhancing the effectiveness of both teaching and learning.

Clyde Chitty
Birmingham,
December 1994.

Preface

This book was mostly written in 2 busy years, when I was school teaching 3 days a week and training teachers 2 days a week. It was difficult finding training materials rigorous enough for a post-graduate course and useful enough for practical school situations. I ended up writing many of my own materials, and was lucky to be able to test these out on student teachers and on experienced colleagues in my own and other schools. To supplement the materials I produced, I looked for books that would help with research and teaching. Many of these I have not only noted but described and quoted in detail. I'd like this book to be used in as many ways as possible, but if readers use it for no more than a guide to other books, I would have no complaints.

My colleagues and pupils will be happy to to say that I am still learning to teach, and I hope to carry on doing so. There is a mystique surrounding training, as though trainers have access to some secret theories invisible to practising teachers. By addressing this book to students, teachers and trainers alike, I hope to reduce the mystery and bring these groups together, supporting the professsional development of them all.

Julian Stern
London, December 1994

CHAPTER 1

Introduction

This book is three things: a guide to researching in schools, a guide to teaching, and a guide to schools and schooling in Britain. It can be used either as a self-study guide (for example by teachers in Independent Schools who have not done the PGCE or BEd), or as a supporting text for specific courses (such as the PGCE). Much of it was originally written to be used by people involved in the initial training of teachers, where that training had a school-based (rather than wholly theoretical or HE based) focus. The rest was originally written for in-service training of experienced teachers in schools. To help with research, a detailed annotated bibliography is included, intended to save time searching through libraries, and library indexes, whilst also stimulating well-focused further reading. The aim of the book is to help teachers to become critical and self-aware, prepared to learn about themselves, about the pupils and schools they work with, and about the education and social system as a whole. Teaching is a stressful, skilful, difficult profession, and I would want anyone who used this book to judge it by its ability to be helpful in the practical school situations faced every day by overworked teachers.

The examples and illustrations used are drawn from, and are applicable to, a very wide variety of schools and subjects. This reflects the author's varied experience of teaching and training, in mainstream and special schools, colleges, HE, and in voluntary groups, teaching children and adults everything from practical skills such as playing the piano or putting up wallpaper, to academic subjects like History and Philosophy.

There are 15 chapters, in four broad categories:

(A) *The teacher as researcher* – All teachers have to be prepared to learn. On courses, whether PGCEs, MAs, or the regular in-service training courses in schools, teachers are expected to do systematic research into education. This first section is a guide to different ways of studying, and is intended to give ideas and advice to all researchers, not just those new to teaching.

(B) *The teacher in the classroom* – An average teacher will spend less than half of their working time in the classroom, but that time is so important that many believe that nothing else matters. Certainly, being an effective classroom practitioner gives more teachers more job satisfaction than any other aspect of the profession.

(C) *The teacher outside the classroom* – Work done outside the classroom is also essential. This section includes many of the issues that are often dealt with outside the classroom, but of course the division between this section and the previous section is rather arbitrary: many issues, such as display, or bullying policies, could go in either section.

(D) *Different perspectives on education* – This section complements and supplements the other three sections. It contains a selection of notes on books that I have found useful. Some are most useful for research, some for classroom practice, some for work outside the classroom. As the title suggests, they are not all written from the same perspective, and are offered here as examples of some of the huge selection of publications available. The comments are purely personal, and are not intended to be any weighty academic judgements.

Section A

THE TEACHER AS RESEARCHER

'Chieftains who ask the wrong questions always hear the wrong answers' (Wes Roberts, *Leadership Secrets of Attila the Hun,* 1989)

CHAPTER 2

Principles of Research

What is Research For?

We expect children to learn: so must schools. Research is always being done in schools – although most of it is not called research, but 'inspection' or 'appraisal' or 'policy documents' or 'school development plans' or 'annual reviews' or whatever. The research done by students, teachers and those on courses, can be part of this whole system of self-analysis, supporting the development of the school. Similarly, research done outside the school is always influencing schools – whether in the form of National Curriculum documents or interesting ideas brought back from conferences. The whole education system is fed by, and feeds itself on, different types of educational research. All students and teachers can contribute to this understanding. Educational research should help people become better teachers. There was a time when much research was separated from schools in such a way as to obscure any connection with the practice of teaching. Moves both within academic research and within training have changed matters, so that most research required of students and teachers is clearly relevant to their experiences as teachers. Good research, incorporating reference to both theory and practice (which need never be seen as opposed to each other), will help make an even more effective teacher, and will help make a teaching career, too.

The bad news – Inexperienced researchers (however experienced they are as teachers) may make mistakes if they are not given suitable guidance, and the blame may land on others. We all want to avoid disasters: a vivid description of the misbehaviour of a named child of a member of the Governing Body, an unguarded quotation from a member of staff about what they really think of the Head, a savage critique of a department whose members are facing redeployment. These are all examples of errors that might be avoided, for example, by a careful consideration of 'confidentiality'. Clear guidance and monitoring, and making staff available for consultation, may help avoid some disasters.

The good news – Schools all need good quality research. They may pay thousands to consultants, they have to pay thousands for OFSTED, and they may appoint people on high salaries to help analyse and develop aspects of the school's work. Schools taking students and having staff doing part-time degrees are able to make use of the research skills of enthusiastic and committed students, supported by HE institutions. Having researchers on the staff is an effective and inexpensive way of tapping in to considerable expertise.

Ethics and Professionalism

Sociologist Martin Bulmer wrote: 'While truth is good, respect for human dignity is better, even if in some circumstances this means that it is not possible to carry out research' (Mann, 1983). A second warning: 'Studying a teacher...at work with his group is regarded as a grossly improper idea, not as a project that might be helpful to society' (Alexander Mitscherlich, *Society Without the Father: A Contribution to Social Psychology*, 1963, 1969, p.24). The ethics of research can be linked to the principles of professionalism: anything unethical to a researcher would probably also be unprofessional. Researchers for example should use diplomacy and tact, and should be sensitive to the effects their research will have on the people and institutions being studied. They should avoid manipulating or deceiving people, and should minimise stress imposed and any invasion of privacy. It is important to discuss what is regarded as ethical or professional at an early stage of research. The following is a personal list of the kinds of issues that might be discussed:

● Being a teacher involves listening, talking to, and being with pupils as they grow up and teachers and other staff as they go about their work. But it is a special kind of relationship that develops. We must listen (and talk) in a different way from how we would listen/talk to friends. We have an obligation not to bully, manipulate, ignore, or otherwise treat pupils or colleagues as if they were our friends!

● As teachers, we are not professional educational consultants, or social workers or medics. Teachers should aim to be good at teaching, and should avoid bad or unprofessional advice. Poor advice (to colleagues

T

as to pupils) can do more damage than noncommittal, good quality, 'listening'. Research should therefore dig deep, and should analyse. It should 'listen'. It is inevitably critical, in the sense that it takes nothing for granted, but it should not be a tirade of personal or institutional criticism, full of uncompromising advice (saying what is 'good' or 'bad') to colleagues or pupils.

- When difficult issues come up within the school, we also need to remember that teachers in schools shouldn't arbitrarily (i.e. without a school policy on the issue) try to impose their own convictions on schools concerning politics, philosophy or religion. It is worth noting that if we talk about our beliefs, even if they are the same as those of the pupils, we have started imposing our views, however gently we express them. Teachers are influential adults – however uncertain that influence is! The research done in school, and the research report presented to a school, should therefore not be an attempt to manipulate people in the school, though it may, of course, attempt to highlight key issues that have been forgotten or hidden.

- The education system is independent of the interests of an individual teacher or school, so we are not wholly free to 'make up our own rules'. If we can't follow the rules of professional conduct, or the rules set down by the government, LEA, or school, we shouldn't really be teachers in that school. Research should be set in that context. Again, I would stress that research *should* be able to be controversial (indeed, bland research is probably no good at all); what is not needed is research that, in its process or in its conclusions, fails to respect the rules of the institution or the profession.

Confidentiality and Anonymity

Standard research practice is to leave people and institutions unnamed, or to give them pseudonyms. In exceptional cases, for example with an 'expert witness', researchers may cite the words of actual individuals but if they do, they must always check that the individual is willing to be quoted at the time of the interview or questionnaire and then confirm the actual words with the respondent before including them in the report. Researchers may refer to a school, for example, as 'a mixed, comprehensive, C of E school in an Outer London Borough, 80% of pupils coming from surrounding estates and about 20% commuting from neighbouring Boroughs'. There is no need to name the school. Similarly, when referring to people, there is no need to name them. Information may need further disguise, because it should be treated as far as possible as confidental – and it must be confidential if any confidentiality is promised to respondents. For example, if a researcher says that 'a head of Science' is very critical of 'a head of Art', it wouldn't take Sherlock Holmes to work out who said what. Perhaps 'middle managers have strong views on the work of their peers' would be as much as I'd recommend anyone saying. As with all such ethical issues, monitoring and sometimes careful guidance is an important role of a research supervisor, mentor or tutor.

Choice of Topic

Choosing a topic may seem easy, but should be difficult, or at least important. A topic is more than a title. It is a 'research question', tightly framed, suggestive of the kind of evidence it seeks, and arrived at often after much hard work and deliberation. It should be related to course objectives, if part of a course, it should be supportable by an appropriate academic framework (i.e. there should be supporting literature on the topic), and it should be supportable by the appropriate tutors or mentors or school(s) in which the research will take place. Researchers may come with clear ideas about what they would like to study: in such cases, tutors or schools may just provide methodological pointers. Other researchers may be open to suggestion. A few may even seem to say 'it isn't my job to choose a topic: just tell me what to do'. In such cases, schools can stimulate good research by nudging students towards issues that are central to the *school's* current concerns, so that the research, when done, has built-in relevance.

It is worth stressing the idea of the topic being an argument, not just a survey of current practice. An educational argument is a piece of work that sets out to persuade – that provides evidence for or against a particular point of view or theory. Researchers get no credit for stating the obvious – e.g. 'lesson planning is really useful', or 'mixed ability teaching is very demanding'. In fact, you can often have more fun arguing for something that seems at first sight to be totally ridiculous – as Ivan Illich did (Illich, 1970, 1971), where he argued that schools prevent education taking place, or as Mary Warnock did in Special Children, No.61, November/December 1992, where she argued that her own, famous, Warnock Report was 'naïve to the point of idiocy'. The argument should be clear and logical. 'Clear' means that each part of the report is relevant – if necessary, just add a couple of sentences at the start or end of the section saying, 'In this section, I have demonstrated the relevance of...', etc. 'Logical' means that you should avoid contradicting yourself.

Whereas any (reasonable) view can be put forward in your work, you should put it forward in such a way that it is obvious you have thought about other views. There is clearly a debate, for example, on mixed-ability or setting in school. If you write about the topic mentioning only one side of the debate, or mentioning both sides but only taking account of evidence from one side in your research, then you will leave yourself open to the accusation of bias or propagandising.

Access to Information

Student teachers and other researchers may have an unsophisticated understanding of the availability of information and how freely certain information can be used. They need to strike a balance between their hopes for completely unfettered access to data (and any accompanying expectation that 'the school' should supply this on demand), and the natural caution schools may have with respect to the uses to which such information may be put. For example, information will inevitably be gleaned from pupils' comments in lessons or staff comments in staffrooms, but the school may wish to limit the uses to which such comments are made. As long as the school is open about what can or cannot be used, there should be few problems.

It is often useful to compare schools. Many researchers have done excellent comparisons of two schools – whether on strategies for dealing with bullying, homework, special needs, or whatever. It would be useful if each school thought about the possibility of allowing access to another school – perhaps a feeder school, or one involved in a consortium, or sharing a foundation – and allowing people from other schools access to your school.

Audience and Ownership

Researchers should be aware that they are likely to be writing for (at least) two audiences – for example, an HE institution, a publisher and a school – and that some alterations may need to be made to make the report appropriate to each audience. Some alterations will simply be matters of style (for example, footnotes or bibliographies may not be wanted by schools), others will be more substantial. For example, if research is done in two schools, it might be better to limit the information given to each school about the other school.

CHAPTER 3

Methods of Research

Acknowledgement and Use of Prior Knowledge and Experience

Experienced teachers don't have a monopoly of knowledge of education. Students and new teachers have a great deal of prior knowledge of education (as pupils and, frequently, as teachers, youth leaders, in personnel, etc., as well as through prior reading), of which use should be made. The following are examples of ways of gaining access to this prior learning, and the learning gleaned from the first few days of observation in a school. Such discussions are particularly useful in the initial stages of defining research questions, and are especially effective when done in small groups (pairs or trios).

- We all have previous experiences of education, good and bad, which influenced us. What are they? The biggest influences are more likely to be human than written. Identify who has been most influential. The person may have been from your childhood, or from last week; they may be a teacher or a member of your family.

- For me, there is also a set of 'documents' – books, TV and film – which has influenced me in different ways. What are the documents that have been influential to you, and why? I have, incidentally, produced a list of 'My Top Ten Favourite Education Documents', ranging from Michael Marland to Grange Hill. (Listed in Chapter 14.) Perhaps experienced teachers might work out their own top ten. This may help researchers realise that reading is not only done on courses!

- What have you already learned about children? What have you learned about schools? What have you learned about teachers? (Or, what are the most *important* things you have learned?)

- What has surprised you most during the course or job so far? What has been the most puzzling?

- What aspects of the teacher's job appeal to you most? Least?

- What do you think you most need to learn about now?

- Think of the lesson you can remember as being the most difficult or satisfying of the ones you have so far observed either before the course started, or during the first few days in your new school. Explain (briefly) what the lesson was about, and why you thought it difficult or satisfying. (It may be that one lesson was both the most difficult and the satisfying lesson.)

Primary Sources: Qualitative and Quantitative Data

Primary or first-hand research is potentially exciting and motivating. It must be done. However, it can also be time consuming (for researchers and for other staff), and, if done badly, invalid and intrusive. You may look for qualitative or quantitative data. Where qualitative data are wanted – an understanding, for example, of people's feelings or perspectives, or an analysis of all the complexities of, say, the use of role playing in school – researchers may get a wealth of information. Try not to get overwhelmed. An open-ended interview, for example, lasting 20 minutes, can generate 20 or 30 pages of transcriptions. Many researchers prefer to search out quantitative data. They are often drawn to questionnaires given out in large numbers to dozens or even hundreds of pupils or teachers. There is a certain comfort in numbers, but if the questions are inappropriately worded, or if the researcher doesn't have sufficient statistical skills to analyse the significance of quantitative data, it will all be a massive waste of time. It is best of course to search out both qualitative and quantitative data.

Clear-headed decisions need to be taken linking data collection to the precise research questions. The link is made by the principle of 'fitness for purpose': whether or not the data are fit for the purpose of the study.

- Where qualitative data (i.e. data that can't be put into figures) have been found, the argument will be supported or illuminated by quotation. What is looked for here is the ability to extract relevant information from the mass of data collected. Data doesn't always 'speak for itself'.

Personal experience provides much qualitative data. It can and should be included in research, though the researcher shouldn't slip into 'proof by anecdote'. (If you are working on bullying, how have you dealt with it or seen it dealt with? If you are working on differentiated learning, what sort of techniques and materials have you used?) The ability to reflect critically on both positive and negative experience is a particular feature of many studies using qualitative data.

- If quantitative data are used, researchers should avoid vague terms such as 'often', or 'several' if they can be more specific. For example, it's better to say that marriage was mentioned by 15 out of 20 girls and 3 out of 20 boys when talking about their future than to use vague terms like 'many' or 'few'. With numerical data, it will often, of course, be convenient to summarise these in tables, graphs and charts. Perhaps the best test of data presentation is to show it to someone who is not familiar with the topic to check its comprehensibility.

- The collection of quantitative data may at first appear straightforward and, for this reason, appealing. Given the limited time usually available for research, it is worth sounding a note of caution. For quantitative data to be processed effectively, avoiding the trap of attaching spurious reliability to findings, large data sets may be required, along with a thorough understanding of statistical techniques.

Classroom Observation

People may observe classrooms for a variety of reasons. They may be doing research, they may be trying to learn how to teach, they may be inspecting or judging pupils or teachers, they may be helping out friends or colleagues. In other sections of this book there is guidance on various aspects of observation – for example, in Chapter 6 there is guidance on looking at learning, and in Chapter 12 there is guidance on what inspectors may be looking for. This section is just a brief guide, bringing together some of the principles of observation implicit elsewhere in the book.

- Completely neutral or objective observation is impossible, for at least two reasons. The observer will affect the thing being observed, however 'invisible' they try to be. (Teachers as well as pupils tend to behave differently when observed.) And what you 'see' will depend on your knowledge and perspective. For example, how you 'see' a pupil disagreeing with a teacher will depend on your views on or expectations about the authority of teachers.

- Given the first point, it is often better (with the prior approval of the teacher and if possible the pupils) to 'muck in'. Having an extra helper in the class is generally less scary than having a dummy at the back of the room. 'Mucking in' also allows you to test out tentative conclusions, by asking pupils what they are doing. Avoid the temptation, of course, to take over the whole class.

- Practise different ways of recording what you observe, and use the method you find most effective. Some people like to write nothing until after the observation, some make general notes, some have headings under which they make more focused notes, some have sophisticated schedules incorporating tick-lists and precise timings, some do audio- or video-recordings or take photographs. All have advantages and disadvantages. I prefer focused notes, or a combination of unstructured notes and audio-recording. It depends on your skills, and the purpose of the observation. This leads on to the next point.

- Decide what sort of things you are looking for. If you are doing research, this may be obvious; if you are sitting in on a friend's lesson, to give them a bit of moral support, this may be much less obvious. A simple, if-all-else-fails, set of things to look for would be: look for those things that worked well, and those things that could be improved. Even this simple list gets complicated if you try to clarify it, saying whether you are looking primarily at what individual pupils are doing, or groups of pupils, or the teacher, or the environment, or the structure of the lesson, or oral work, or behaviour, or learning, or whatever. Decide in advance, but be prepared to be flexible.

- Try to observe at least twice. Whatever you are looking for, your evidence is likely to be more meaningful if it covers two or more periods of observation. Any single observation may be unduly affected by peculiar circumstances.

- Give feedback after the observation. Tell the teacher something about what you saw – if possible, starting with the best bits, and always being constructive. If possible, tell the pupils too. If you won't get a chance after the observation, then you might try saying something like 'thanks for letting me work with you today; I've really enjoyed seeing you work so hard on this topic'.

- Analyse the observation in as interesting a way as you can. Bland descriptions are very little good for anyone, for any purpose. What have you seen that is new? What evidence have you found for or against a theory? What has the observation inspired you to do? Observation should provide rich information. If it doesn't, it hasn't been done right!

Secondary Sources: Documents in School, LEA and Libraries

Researchers are expected to make good use of secondary sources (relevant literature) which will inform and contextualise practical issues. The school will have much written information that would be of use. Often, there will be a staff library. How much access researchers will have to this is, of course, up to the school. HE institutions' own libraries form an essential resource, along with libraries in teachers' centres or in LEA offices. Computerised catalogues may allow researchers to look up authors, or titles, or topics. Bookshops should also be useful. They tend to be more up to date than libraries. If one book is liked or trusted, its bibliography may be the source of further titles. Researchers should not underestimate apparently 'ephemeral' reading, too. Newspaper articles (especially from the *TES* and education sections in daily papers), handouts or policy documents, notices in staff rooms, television programmes, etc., can be useful illustrative material and, like journal articles and books, should be properly acknowledged.

Demonstrating reading doesn't mean copying out chunks of a book or policy document, but referring to them to back up or complement the theoretical or practical work done. For example 'The results of my survey suggest that Willis (1977) underestimated the significance of gender in the formation of peer groups, but that he was right to concentrate on the influence of work.'

The most often recommended system for references and bibliographies is the Harvard system. This system is useful, and often essential, but causes unnecessary worry amongst researchers. Early reminders, and keeping good records of everything read, may help researchers meet academic referencing requirements.

Currency: Awareness of Current Government and Local Issues

Good work on current affairs can satisfy the need for research to be fresh and immediately relevant, and there are several ways of covering such issues through a course or, adapted, when doing individual research.

● Each week, one course member could be nominated to read the *TES* and/or *Education Guardian*, and give a 15 minute report to the whole group the next week. This could either be a broad survey of several issues, or a fuller account of one issue that the person feels is particularly important. If the tutor or school has a notice-board, key articles could be pinned up, week by week, to produce a diary of the year. Perhaps if key articles were mounted on card, with comments or questions added, they could also be used by other staff in the school for INSET, as well as by other students in their research. Most current educational issues could also be discussed by pupils in PSE lessons.

- A more ambitious activity, which could also provide a great deal of support to research throughout the year, would be a scrap-book. Each course member could choose a topic – either a free choice, or perhaps from a list provided by the tutor – and keep a file or scrap-book of relevant articles from the *TES, Education Guardian,* or other papers and magazines, along with accounts or recordings of radio or television programmes. During seminars throughout the year, the tutor might ask one person to present some of the information in their scrap-book, relevant to the topic being covered. These scrap-books could be used as the basis of further research, and could also, of course, be used by schools (and tutors) for INSET.

- A third style of research would involve pupils. Each course member could be set the task of preparing a current educational issue for use in a PSE lesson (or, if relevant, in a subject lesson). Recent useful topics might be whether pupils should sit SATs, how to tackle racism in schools, funding arrangements and spending cuts, anti-bullying campaigns, integration of pupils with Special Educational Needs, streaming and setting, opting out, sex education, worship and religion in schools, and so on. This approach would also satisfy the need to cover PSE in schools in more detail, and if the course members were to use the opportunity to record the lesson, or use some sort of survey technique, they could produce some excellent material for further research.

Theory and Practice

It is tempting to say 'This is all very good in theory, but in practice...' . Researchers should avoid this pitfall. If a 'theory' is irrelevant or wrong in practice, then it's a bad theory. You can use the word 'elegant' to describe a fine looking but bad theory, but perhaps only if you are being sarcastic. All theories are theories about the world, and a 'good' theory is

Printed on 12 December 2007 at 15:19

Journey Itinerary

Outward Journey

Date:	**12 December 2007**			
From:	**WELWYN GDN CITY**	Depart:	**15:23**	
To:	**CRICKLEWOOD**	Arrive:	**16:35**	Duration:	**01 hours 12 mins**

Number of Changes: **2**

Depart	Date	Time	Arrive	Date	Time	Operating Company
WELWYN GDN CITY	**12/12/2007**	**15:23**	**HIGHBURY & ISLTN**	**12/12/2007**	**16:00**	**First Capital Connect**
HIGHBURY & ISLTN	**12/12/2007**	**16:05**	**LONDON ST PANCRS**	**12/12/2007**	**16:09**	**Underground**
LONDON ST PANCRS	**12/12/2007**	**16:25**	**CRICKLEWOOD**	**12/12/2007**	**16:35**	**First Capital Connect**

The information printed here was valid at date and time of printing.

a theory that tells us something about the world. It can help clarify or challenge what we think we 'know' or 'see'. Does the theory (or, more likely, theories) studied during the course match the practice observed or taken part in? If it does, good. If it doesn't, then find a theory that does. Researchers can as necessary invent their own theory. Indeed, this can be at the heart of research and development − being engaged in critical and informed *theorising*, rather than learning *about* theory.

CHAPTER 4

Forms of Research

The Social Context of a School

Most HE institutions promote the idea of involving students, early in the course, with some sort of study of the social context within which education takes place. The intention is to help students avoid the (understandable) mistake of thinking that all they need to do is watch a 'good' teacher teach, in order to become a good teacher themselves. They need a range of experience including learning about the range of social, political, cultural, economic and environmental factors that can impinge on the operation of the school.

Many people start to get to know the area around the school by simply walking about. This is what many teachers do before an interview, for example. However, if you wish to encourage a more systematic approach to 'walking about', you may want to think about a Community Trail. Here are two plans:

● *Community Trail I:* The school organises it. The advantage of this is that people in the school are likely to have considerable knowledge of the community. Produce a route map, taking students to the most interesting areas round the school, and set accompanying tasks – e.g. describe the different types of housing, list all the religious and community groups on the trail, analyse the ethnicity of shops and restaurants, study public indicators of wealth and poverty, find leisure facilities suited to school children. Schools might think of other tasks to set, suited to their own communities.

● *Community Trail II:* Students or newcomers to the school organise it. The advantage of this is that it gets people into 'teacher mode' straight away. They may design a trip around the community, with accompanying worksheets of tasks suited to pupils in, e.g., Year 7 or Year 10. Perhaps some of the group could organise a trip for the others (role-playing 12 year olds). The write-up may include an analysis of what makes a good school trip.

Other more substantial pieces of research can be done around the school. Community studies can specialise on particular aspects of the locality, such as language diversity, ethnicity, uses of local facilities (including, for example, a river or park or monument), a comparison of markets in different parts of the Borough, housing, religion, employment opportunities, famous people who have lived in the area, youth culture, refugees/immigration and schooling, the impact of transport on the school, and many others.

One possible outcome of a study of the community around the school is a display that could be used in school. This itself can become a resource in different curriculum subjects. For example, a study of shops in different parts of the Borough could stimulate lesson plans on shop names in English and French (MFL), designing waterproof shop signs (Science), or a day-in-the-life story (English). A study of famous people could stimulate lesson plans on two contrasting artists (Art), heroes and obituaries (RE), routes (Geography). (See also the section on Display in Chapter 12.)

Studying the School Itself

Studying the community around the school may be important, but most education research will of course happen within schools. Schools themselves may help generate ideas about what could be researched in the school. Many schools have asked researchers to look at issues in their school development plans, or to do research in preparation for some whole-school INSET. Researchers may of course already have strong ideas about what they would like to research, and the school can advise on the appropriateness of these ideas.

An enquiry could be a largely document-based investigation, for example on school (and LEA) policies, homework arrangements, behaviour management, language across the curriculum, Records of Achievement (ROA) and reports, after-school clubs, marketing the school, use of the library, or other such topics. Document-based research might be seen as a pilot study for a larger scale piece of research. Larger projects may include not only research but also 'development'. 'Research and Development' work – popular in industry – makes sense for schools: the idea of putting 'development' into the title is to make absolutely clear the professional implications of research. Research on homework might include proposals for guidance on homework to be used by teachers, as well as academic and school based research on the topic. Research on counselling might involve developing counselling skills as well as learning about counselling skills. Research on behaviour in the classroom might involve producing a video of pupils role-playing typical classroom situations and discussing them afterwards, which could even be used for future courses.

A Possible Structure of a Research Report

This is just a suggestion, based in part on recommendations made to A-Level sociologists and PGCE students. Do please read this section, but only make use of it if it is useful to you: various courses provide their own preferred formats, lengths (the word-guide here is for a report of between 6,000 and 10,000 words: a common recommended length), bibliographies, and so on. Methodology is important. As well as finding out about some aspect of education, a report of research should help you find out about finding out. This means understanding how to research, what problems and advantages there are in the methods you use, whether you believe that individual people's feelings are more important than the influences of society (or vice versa), and so on.

Introduction (altogether, perhaps 800–1250 words)

After the cover, front page, and table of contents, you may be expected to provide a 200–300 word abstract (summary of key findings) and a rationale (which includes a statement of your reasons for choosing the topic and reasons for choosing the methods you have chosen). These, and/or the introduction, may refer to arguments and theories placing your research in the context of existing research and literature, and mentioning personal interest, contacts, experience or concerns that led you to this choice. The introduction should also define the central issues of your research, either in the form of general aims or (preferably) specific hypotheses. Keep this section relatively brief; it's not the place for an extended discussion of educational theory (which should be in the 'content' section). Its purpose is to demonstrate that you have thought through the intellectual and professional implications of your choice of topic.

Also include here the methods of your enquiry, saying how you came to select them. In doing this, it's quite appropriate to talk about approaches that you considered but rejected, giving your reasons. You should also write about the strengths and weaknesses of the methods that you use, whether primary (i.e. first hand) or secondary (i.e. read in books). Do not get involved in a detailed *assessment* of what you were able to find out, as this is more appropriate for the later sections. Remember, though, that 'methods' include your broad approach to educational research: do you think that individual feelings are most influential in the classroom, or social forces; do you think people are driven by natural impulses, or are they infinitely malleable; can schools make a real difference, or are homes, classes, the media, or the government the main determinants of success or failure; etc.

Content (3500–6000 words)

This is the big chunk – the bit that shows how much you've *read* and *researched*. (As a rough guide, the first and third sections are the ones that show how much you *understand*.) Some of the 'content' section may be in the form of a video, drama production, or whatever. If you take this option, I recommend that you include one or two thousand words of description with your video, etc., explaining what went on, as well as, of course, a full introduction and conclusion sections.

The content section is likely to include a selective review of related work. It is necessary to keep a firm control here. If your study concerns the educational opportunities of an ethnic group for example, do not rewrite a textbook chapter on the whole history of ethnicity in Britain. Choose only those elements relevant to your research focus. If your topic is not in the mainstream of educational research, you should say here what use you have been able to make of related ideas, research and theories.

You will also include your own main findings. The structure of this section will, of course, depend on the nature of your enquiry. You will probably need to introduce some further sub-headings to organise the presentation of material. You can get away with keeping the information in this section fairly descriptive if, and only if, you include plenty of analysis in the 'conclusion' section. However, I would recommend that most of the detailed analysis is here, and not all saved up for the conclusion. Somewhere, here or in the conclusion, you will need full-blown analysis, detailed discussion, comparison with other research, theoretical arguments and the evaluation of the success of your methodology and status of your conclusions.

Conclusion and Evaluation (1700–2750 words)

The evaluation of your enquiry's findings is an important element of any report. This section should contain your assessment of the information you have been able to gather and a discussion of its strengths and weaknesses. A thorough examination of the work you have done can help you produce a successful piece of work even if the study was flawed or incomplete. Your conclusions are likely to be in the form of relatively cautious suggestions rather than firm statements. If, however, your study indicates some ideas for subsequent research, even if it is quite tentative in itself, do mention these possible extensions.

The evaluation should also include your judgement of the methods of research that you employed. If your study includes primary research, interpret the significance of your findings, for example in terms of the sample size, and its representativeness. Mention also any biases that might have affected what you have been able to discover. In short, it's better to show yourself aware of any shortcomings in the study – if you don't, then others will conclude that you have not noticed them.

References (as long as it needs to be: not usually counted towards the word count)

Many institutions recommend the Harvard system for written references. All references to books, articles, etc., should be marked in the text by the author's surname and the date of publication, with full details in the bibliography. List all sources of information (e.g. newspaper articles, staff handbooks, etc), not just the books. My annotated bibliography, later in this book, uses the Harvard system.

You may also wish to add an appendix or appendices, e.g. with copies of raw data or interview transcripts.

Note – *please* – that this was just an example of a possible structure. There are a million appropriate structures.

Examples of Research

Types of Project

Here are some forms or examples of research that extend or adapt the more conventional techniques given in many textbooks. This list can be used to stimulate interest in, and imaginative use of, research techniques.

- Get someone to take photos of a class at regular intervals (e.g. every minute for 15 minutes), and use the photos afterwards in interviews with the teacher and a couple of the pupils.

- Research a topic such as bullying and use the findings to help plan a year assembly on the topic.

- Pick the worst book you've ever read on education, and prove it wrong, using evidence for the school.

- Two researchers could visit each other's lessons. Each could suggest to the other a (good or bad) aspect of their work that could be researched and improved.

- Plan a trip to Kew Gardens, as the centre-piece of research on, e.g., experiential learning, or cross-curricular work, or whatever.

- Work shadow the Librarian, or the Schoolkeeper, or the Office Manager, as the foundation of work on alternative perspectives in the school.

- Create a model 'menu' of homework, appropriate for a Year 7 pupil, and compare this to the homework actually set for a Year 7 pupil during a randomly chosen week.

- Get all the pupils in a class to write down all the people – real and fictional – they can remember having studied or found out about since they joined the school. This can be very revealing for anyone researching the gap between what teachers and pupils think is being studied, or the under-representation of certain groups in the curriculum.

- Take a photo of a whole class group, and use the photo (in another school) as the basis of a discussion with staff or pupils, about what expectations they might have of individual pupils in the class.

Types of Questions

How questions are asked can affect the quality and quantity of answers given. Here are some strategies:

- Keep simple questions simple. 'To what racial or ethnic group do you feel you belong?' might get a myriad of unanalysable results. Rather, write 'To which of these ethnic or racial groups do you feel you belong?', followed by a list (e.g. taken from LEA statistics, or from the Census) ending with 'Other – Please state…'.

- Allow for simple yet useful answers to complex questions. 'What do you think of school?' may produce lots of rather uninformative answers (e.g. 'all right'). Why not write out several statements about school (e.g.

'School is very important for giving qualifications' or 'The most important thing about school is having fun') and get respondents to circle a number ranging from 1 to 5, where 1 means 'agree strongly' and 5 'disagree strongly'.

- Encourage multiple answers to important questions. For example, 'What are the three things you like most about homework?' should get a fuller response than 'What do you like about homework?'

- Allow some room for extended answers and comments on the survey. A last question might be 'Do you wish to say anything else about bullying, or about this survey into bullying?'

- If you use several different research techniques, questions may link them. If you interview someone who has done a questionnaire for you, why not ask 'You said this on the questionnaire...What exactly did you mean?'.

- Try to pilot all questions: try them out on at least one person, and ask them whether they make sense. Questions that make sense to *you* may not make sense to someone else, of a different age or experience.

- A small number of good questions is more useful than a large number of bad questions. The Census, done by the government every 10 years (and taking several years to analyse), asks only about a dozen questions. Most effective questionnaires ask between six and 15 questions.

CHAPTER 5

Glossary of Key Terms for Researchers

Case study: An in-depth study of a single person or a single institution. This may gain over broader studies in depth or meaningfulness, but lose in generalisability. Case studies are often seen as more manageable by inexperienced researchers, though such researchers should be aware of the difficulty of drawing general conclusions from a single case study.

Causation: A cause is something that has an effect. Causes may of course be more or less important. Investigating causation is often the central task of research. It is difficult to prove a single cause of anything; however, it is realistic to assume a researcher could find evidence for something being one possible cause of another thing. (See also 'correlation'.)

Content analysis: A way of quantifying aspects of the media, or of social situations. The researcher constructs a set of categories, and counts the frequency with which each category is observed. They may, for example, count the number of women and men who appear in school textbooks, or the number of times different categories of pupils 'misbehave' in lessons. Constructing relevant and unambiguous categories is of course vital.

Correlation: When two variables (e.g. class and exam results) go up or down together, they are said to be correlated. Be wary of treating correlations as proof of causation. For example, there may be a correlation between the rise in exam results and the rise in the sales of trainers, but no one would think one caused the other. Finding correlations is often the first stage in the analysis of quantitative research. It should not be the only form of analysis.

Hypothesis: A provisional statement that formulates the idea to be tested by research. It should not be too 'obvious' (see the section on choice of topic, above), and should allow for evidence or proof both for and against it.

Manageability: A manageable study is one that can yield a sufficient quantity and quality of data on which to base valid and reliable conclusions. It is easy for a piece of research to be too ambitious (and therefore unmanageable) in its methods of data collection. Common causes of unmanageability are having a huge topic (e.g. an analysis of children's learning), having too many variables (e.g. an analysis of the effects of class, ethnicity, and gender on Year 7 and Year 10 pupils), and having too many sources of information (e.g. an analysis of anti-bullying strategies in five schools).

Observation: This refers to looking at or listening to people, either while joining in their activities (participant observation) or whilst an outsider to the activity (non-participant observation). Work out in advance what you intend observing and the framework guiding the observation. Note, however, that it is unethical and illegal to make secret recordings of people without first asking their permission.

Pilot: A pilot study is a small-scale trial of the research you intend to do. This is a particularly good idea, especially if you are going to use a technique such as questionnaires, which, if poorly written, will provide no valid information at all. Research done early in a course can all be regarded as pilot studies for the later research.

Primary Sources of Information: Primary sources of information are ones found or witnessed by you the researcher. If you do a questionnaire, the data provided will be primary sources of information for you. Original research doesn't always include primary data, but it is normally an essential component.

Qualitative: Qualitative research is that which is difficult or inappropriate to put into numbers. Perhaps you will do an in-depth interview with a pupil: what they say could be vital, but would not be quantifiable. Qualitative research can be particularly complex and meaningful, but may be difficult to analyse and report.

Quantitative: Quantitative research comes up with numbers. Often popular with researchers, because it can be easy to analyse, and it lends itself to clear reporting. However, be aware that numbers may look more valid and reliable than they really are.

Questions: A questionnaire is a written list of questions. An interview is a spoken set of questions, and may be structured (all the questions written out in advance), semi-structured or focused, or unstructured (like a conversation). Questions in either questionnaires or interviews may be closed (with a limited number of possible answers, e.g. 'Do you believe in god?') or open (with any type of answer, e.g. 'What do you think about religion?'). Closed questions are easier to quantify. Open questions can yield more complex answers, which are, however, more difficult to analyse and report.

Reliability: Research exhibiting reliability could be repeated by other researchers, in similar situations, and generate the same results. Reliability is often described in terms of reproducibility or repeatability.

Sampling: A sample is a selection from the whole population (whether the population of the world or the population of a school). A representative sample is one that has the same characteristics, in the same proportion, as the population as a whole. A random sample is one where every member of the population is equally likely to get chosen. One way of making a representative sample is to take a very large random sample, but a small random sample may well not be representative. Quota sampling comprisies dividing the population into separate groups and taking a (random) sample from each of these groups. For example, you may take a random sample of two boys and two girls from each class in the school. In doing research it is vital to acknowledge how (un)representative your sample is of the people you wish to generalise about.

Secondary sources of information: Secondary sources come from other researchers, recorded, for example, in books, articles, television programmes, government statistics, school annual reports, etc. Such sources of information are needed to back up evidence you have found yourself. They can give weight to an argument, and can provide a sound theoretical basis for more practical research.

Triangulation: To increase the dependability of conclusions drawn from research, a researcher may use several methods of collecting data. This is 'triangulation', and it makes results more valid and reliable, as data collected in one way are checked against data collected in another way.

Validity: Valid data, or valid conclusions, represent or measure the phenomena they purport to be representing or measuring. For example, a study into intelligence would be invalid if the only data collected to measure intelligence were exam results, as exam results are affected by many things other than intelligence.

Variable: A measurable aspect of society (or of anything) which may change over time. A researcher who intentionally manipulates variables is doing an experiment; a researcher who looks for different patterns of variables in different situations is using the comparative method, often known as a field experiment. When using variables, the researcher must define each one, and say exactly how it is being used. Inaccurate or sloppy use of variables (e.g. assuming 'middle class' or 'black' are uncontroversial and can be measured just by looking at people) is to be avoided. Important variables in education research include class, gender, ethnicity, achievement, ability, age, family or home circumstances, type of school (e.g. independent, selective, comprehensive, single sex, etc.), type of teaching (e.g. mixed ability, teacher-centred, experiential, etc.), and subject taught.

Section B

THE TEACHER IN THE CLASSROOM

'The best teachers are those who choose deliberately and inventively amongst a repertoire of learning activities, or who can judge when the pupils themselves can choose the strategies most likely to advance their learning.'

(Douglas Barnes, quoted in NCC, 1991)

CHAPTER 6

What Stimulates or Prevents Learning?

Equal Opportunities in Practice

Stimuli and Blocks

Education involves change: 'leading out' new knowledge, understanding and skills. Change can be promoted, or it can be prevented. Teaching is about stimulating learning, and minimising the blocks to learning. Equal opportunities in education means each pupil should be given equal stimulus, or should be helped to overcome equal blocks, in their learning. Equal opportunities is not to do with making every pupil produce the same performance.

Blocks to learning, and stimuli to learning, can come from within the pupil, from the teacher, from other people (family, peer group or friends, people in the same class, etc.), from 'society' (media, political movements, social conditions, etc.), and so on. Because the teacher is just one source of stimulus, it may be that the teacher will have to compensate a pupil for the lack of other stimuli. The teacher may even end up being accused of spending too much energy on a minority of pupils, but if this really is compensating for other conditions it can be justified. For example, if a pupil is ignored by others in the class (or in their family, or in society), the teacher may wish to give them extra attention. This seems reasonable!

What Direct Influence does a Teacher Have?

A teacher may be aware of how they stimulate or block learning themselves. This is quite easy to control if, and only if, the teacher is reflective (thinks about what they have done) and is prepared to be flexible. A teacher may, however, be unconscious of some of the ways they stimulate or block learning. The teacher may be accidentally rude (maybe simply by pronouncing names wrongly), they may be insensitive (perhaps by asking 'what would your parents think of this behaviour?', if the pupil didn't have, or didn't live with, parents), they may talk or look strange or off-putting to the pupils, or they may look or act like someone who is frightening to a pupil (perhaps a parent!). For this reason, teachers need to work out strategies to minimise these unconscious effects on pupils. This can be difficult.

What Else Should Every Teacher Know?

An even more difficult problem is how much the teacher knows about other influences on the pupils. Teachers can't know what it's like being every sort of pupil. Some may know what it's like being female, or working class, or homosexual, or a member of an ethnic minority, or disabled, or having family in prison, or very small, or bereaved, or not understanding English, or having learning difficulties. But not all teachers can (or should) know first hand about all of these experiences. The point is, blocks to learning (and stimuli) are not evenly distributed. Women are more likely than men to be ignored; lesbians and homosexual men are more likely to be pressured to hide their feelings than heterosexuals; the disabled are more likely to be condescended to than the able-bodied; recently bereaved people are more likely to find it difficult to be enthusiastic about learning than others. It is no good to think that we, as teachers, simply need to 'treat all the pupils the same': pupils are not all the same. We may need to try to compensate for blocks to learning that are completely beyond our control.

Giving equal opportunities may, initially, mean giving similar stimulus to all pupils, and avoiding creating barriers to learning. However, as we get to know more about the pupils, giving them equal opportunities may also mean finding ways of overcoming their individual blocks to learning, or compensating for their individual lack of other stimulus. As each pupil is also a member of several groups (e.g. they are male, or working class, or able-bodied, etc.) teachers should find it useful finding out about patterns of treatment of particular groups. This gets us on to the usual topics of equal opportunities – race, gender, class, disability, sexual orientation, and so on. Do not think that these 'categories' are all quite distinct, in need of distinct justification. Do not be tempted to think that there is a fixed list of blocks to learning. The lists given out by institutions, or enshrined in laws, are simply examples (perhaps very significant issues, or politically sensitive issues) of some of the infinite number of issues brought up by the question 'how do we ensure equal opportunities in education?'

Please think it worth while trying to give all pupils equal opportunities – this is what teaching means. Think about any one lesson you have taught, and go over it, trying to work out how the topic was presented, what the subject-matter included, what tasks were required of each pupil, and how each pupil responded. What equal opportunities lessons can be drawn? It is worth discussing each other's lessons in this way. It is sometimes easier looking at equal opportunities as an outsider. Try to do secondary research, too. A list of books I have found useful is in Chapter 14.

Special Educational Needs in the Mainstream Classroom

The phrase SEN is weighted down by legal and political meanings – some of which are explained in my bibliography. (My favourites are listed in Chapter 14.) Special Educational Needs includes pupils who are 'behind' (in some sense) their peers with their learning, unless the lag is a result of having English as a second or subsequent language. A bilingual pupil, with difficulties, should be treated differently (and has another source of extra funding for their education – usually called 'Section 11' funding) to a pupil with other learning difficulties. Of course, the actual help given to bilingual pupils and pupils with SEN could often be very similar. For example, it might be appropriate to give work that is very structured, and which doesn't include only long pieces of extended writing, to some pupils in both categories. Treating bilingual and SEN pupils differently means having distinct referral systems, distinct or at least distinguishable policies or structures to support them, and an awareness of the different needs and likely development of pupils in both categories.

Some schools use the phrase Special Needs (without the Educational). This is sometimes a slip of the pen, sometimes a way of grouping together SEN and Bilingual support, and sometimes a way of including 'gifted' children. 'Gifted' children (yes, I know, all children are gifted, but ..) are those who are significantly *ahead of* (in some sense) their peers. Sometimes the phrase used is 'pupils of marked ability'. Very able pupils may have special needs, i.e. they may need an adapted curriculum to bring out their best efforts.

Schools may therefore have a department of Special Needs, catering for three (or even more) groups: pupils with SEN, bilingual pupils, and gifted pupils.

It is important to point out that good, exciting, relevant, well-resourced, differentiated, lessons will almost inevitably be supportive for pupils with

SEN, and for bilingual and gifted children. There are not *four* ways in which you should teach well (one way for each 'special' category, and one way for 'the rest'), but one way. Avoid the temptation to think, when planning a lesson, that you should first plan for 'the rest', then add an extra or alternative worksheet for each 'special' pupil. This would be appalling, both in terms of your work-load and in terms of the labelling of the 'special' pupils. Your extra work would also often be rejected by its recipients ('why do I have to do this?') or demanded by the others ('why can't we do that sheet?'). Just teach well. To understand some of the key issues in SEN, I would recommend extended study of key texts including school policies (and practices) of whichever schools you have contact with.

Medical Matters

Why are Medical Issues Important?

- Pupils (like teachers) are only human – all too human at times – and therefore are affected by medical conditions which in turn may affect their learning. (It is interesting to debate whether schools are there to develop the whole person, or to encourage learning, or whether the two are inseparable.)

- There has been a move towards the integration into mainstream schools of pupils who had previously been taught separately – in schools, for example, for physically disabled, delicate, hearing- or sight-impaired pupils. Teachers are increasingly likely to teach pupils with a wide variety of medical conditions, with implications for their education.

- It appears that our knowledge of medical issues and our abilities to control medical conditions are increasing. At the same time, controversy continues over the boundaries of the medical. Whether, for example, psychological conditions (such as schizophrenia) are 'medical', whether certain apparent conditions (such as repetitive strain injury) even exist, whether some conditions (such as dyslexia) have a single origin and if so whether it is physical or psychological, and so on. It is worth trying to understand at least some of these issues.

What Should Teachers Do?

- Be sensitive to the possible effects of medical conditions on learning.

Being sensitive doesn't mean being soft: it is no help to someone whose health is 'failing' simply to let them fail academically too! Being sensitive means, for example:
- giving pupils opportunities to explain medical conditions without all their fellow pupils listening in;
- giving practical support, such as seating a hearing-impaired child where they can see the teacher easily;
- avoiding using a medical condition as an excuse, as in 'that's a good piece of work considering your shaky handwriting'.

● Learn about the educational implications of at least some medical conditions. This is a long-term project, because there is a lot to learn, and because our medical knowledge changes so quickly. Learn from pupils and their carers, colleagues, friends, books (e.g. D'Albert, 1989), and television, and, of course, from your own experience. If there is a school nurse or doctor, they should be worth talking to.

● Learn what to do in cases of medical emergency. For some emergencies you may wish to intervene – even if intervention simply involves getting other pupils out of the way. For others you will want to know whom to call for (e.g. a first-aider in the school, an ambulance, or a parent); or you will want to know that you should avoid intervening. Again, learn from pupils and their carers, colleagues, friends, books, television, your own experience, and school nurses or doctors.

Types of Educational Implications of Medical Conditions

Some conditions affect learning directly. Hearing impairment may lead to misunderstanding teacher instructions. (This is one of the most under-diagnosed conditions in pupils: teachers often think the pupil is simply being disobedient, and the pupil may grow to live up to this assumption.) Petit mal epileptic fits may mean a child simply loses concentration and looks blank: they may not realise they have been 'absent'. The teacher may have to repeat instructions or guidance. Pupils with hydrocephalus may have specific learning difficulties in perceptual and spatial judgements, affecting hand/eye co-ordination. A diabetic child may, with too little food or too much exercise, react to their insulin by losing concentration, sweating, becoming more stubborn, crying, shaking, and so on. Some children may have allergic reactions (eczema, asthma, hayfever, etc.) to certain materials – as diverse as pollen, chalk dust, class pets or plants, various foods, or detergent – which may create soreness, itching, headaches, and so on. Pre-menstrual tension may affect moods and concentration. Thyroid conditions may make someone hyperactive.

Some treatments affect learning directly. Cold treatments and anti-histamines can cause drowsiness; anti-depressant drugs can cause lack of concentration; and so on. Non-medical use of drugs can also affect learning directly.

As well as direct effects on learning, many medical conditions have *indirect* effects. A pupil with severe eczema may be self-conscious, and may feel (and may be) rejected by other pupils either because of their appearance or because people wrongly think eczema is infectious. Low self-esteem may result, and children may react to this by being very 'clingy' with adults, or in any number of ways. They may also become manipulative and self centred. ('It is therefore essential to establish a sensible balance between making allowances and giving fair discipline and guidance', D'Albert, 1989.) A pupil with any condition that has led to them taking time off school will not only have lost that part of their education, but may also have problems of rejoining a class or making friends. A pupil with any life-threatening condition (including very common conditions such as asthma) may have a tendency to be fearful or panicky, or unwilling to take risks. A pupil with a condition that involves getting lots of treatment, such as cystic fibrosis, may have difficulties taking responsibility for their own actions or work, and may seem immature, or may try to reject treatments (and people). The social stigma (including discrimination and bullying) attached to conditions such as HIV/AIDS, or physical disfigurement, can affect pupils in a huge number of ways.

Dickens made illness and disability in childhood (such as Tiny Tim in *A Christmas Carol*) a source of pathos. Many people follow his sentimental lead, but teachers should not assume that children themselves behave like Dickens' characters when they are ill, or like Dickens when their fellow pupils are ill.

Infectious Diseases

There is a list of notifiable diseases. If any child (or teacher) is known to have any of these diseases, the school must notify the local authority. So if a child says they think they have mumps or measles, you as a teacher must pass the information on to someone responsible in the school (e.g. the Head). The list of notifiable diseases given in D'Albert (1989) is as follows, but this list may change – and may already have changed. Whereas some diseases (like plague and rabies) are not surprisingly listed, some on the list (like food poisoning) might be ignored by a school as trivial and not worth reporting.

Notifiable diseases: Acute encephalitis; acute poliomyelitis; anthrax; cholera; diphtheria; dysentery (amoebic bacillary); food poisoning;

leprosy; malaria; measles; meningitis; meningococcal septicaemia (without meningitis); mumps; ophthalmia neonatorum; paratyphoid fever; plague; rabies; relapsing fever; rubella (German measles); scarlet fever; smallpox; tetanus; tuberculosis; typhoid fever; viral haemorrhage fever; viral hepatitis; whooping cough; yellow fever. It is worth noting that AIDS is not a notifiable disease.

CHAPTER 7

Organising the Classroom

Introduction: Organise Learning not Teaching

Teachers often feel as though school inspectors are looking at the quality of teaching rather than the quality of learning: teachers feel as though they are performing, not as though they are getting the *pupils* to perform. Similarly, people new to teaching, when they observe classrooms for the first time, tend to look at the teacher and try to work out what magic skills they can learn. Good. But the great magic of teaching is setting up situations in which pupils are trying to learn: it is the *pupils* who make a fine lesson. I was annoyed myself (when my lessons were being observed) that people complimented lessons where I felt I was just 'wandering about' helping pupils more than they complimented lessons where I was 'performing' for the whole class. Arrogance. As if I as a teacher should be judged by my performance, rather than by the performance of the *pupils*. What I've tried to put here, therefore, are ideas on effective learning, with the emphasis on producing lessons that are sufficiently differentiated to cater for all pupils.

Differentiation

Every group of people (however they are selected) are a 'mixed ability' group. This is not a problem. If you see it as a problem, then that's a problem. 'Differentiation' simply means taking account of the mixture of abilities in your lesson. You are the conductor of an orchestra of different instruments: no one goes to a concert to see the conductor alone, or to see the orchestra all playing the same tune on one instrument. Good learning, then, goes on when different pupils are all able to learn. The next few sections look at ways in which teachers can help improve the quality of learning, by attempting to differentiate work done by pupils and, indeed, by teachers.

Planning

● As far as lesson-planning goes, it is impossible to differentiate your lessons if you use just one teaching technique – e.g. just lecture, or if the pupils all just read the same book. Always plan for fast and slow work to be done at the same time, whilst also bringing the class together at significant points; always have 'spare' work ('gap-fillers') to give out in emergencies (see later for more work on emergencies); make the lesson and term plan obvious or visible – e.g. display it on notice-boards.

● The different skills and knowledge of teachers is often overlooked by school departments – even by departments well aware of differences between *pupils*. A general topic introduction can help ensure that each teacher isn't having to repeat the same groundwork done by every other teacher, and that, on key issues (like the dating system used in the Muslim world, or the definition of 'revolution') the whole department is pulling together. This should save work, and help with staff 'differentiation'.

● As well as the introductions to the topics, departments are (rightly) expected to do general teaching plans, often called programmes of work. The 'boxes' way of doing this is a handy way of focusing on key topics. Often, sadly, differentiation can mean pupils having quite different experiences from each other: this can divide a class and make group learning impossible. A *good* curriculum plan can mean that all teachers, and therefore all pupils, have access to the same key concepts, activities, homework, etc. Programmes of work for different courses will include both the 'what' and the 'how' of the course, broken down into appropriate units, and will also demonstrate review procedures – such as a form of regular student and course assessment, incorporating target-setting.

Planning for the Unplanned

Planning for the unplanned, too, is important. Teachers and classes are not easy to predict. What about the video recorder that doesn't work, or the fire-drill that cuts an hour's lesson down to 20 minutes, or the pupil with the nose bleed that needs seeing to, or the short-notice cover lesson for the teacher who has just run out screaming? And how do you plan for such unplanned situations in a way that doesn't negate all the great, sensitive, work you've done with the pupils for the rest of the year? Always have a pile of spare paper, and ideas for what the pupils can write. Ideas include quizzes/puzzles/games, surveys, bribery.

● Quizzes are generally popular: a simple all-purpose format is to write letters of the alphabet down the side of the page, and think of words (related to the subject) to match each letter – e.g. musicians, or countries of the world, or historical figures. Think of your own favoured formats *(before* the unplanned lesson). Try asking the pupils to write a quiz themselves – either for themselves (or their classmates), or for another year group. You may be surprised how enjoyable (and how hard) pupils find writing questions. (Such an exercise also, happily, provides material for the next emergency!)

● Puzzles may be of any kind – again, find your favourite for your pupils, in advance of the emergencies. Examples include word games (e.g. composing sentences that read the same backwards as forwards, such as 'Madam, I'm Adam', or sentences with every word beginning with the same letter, or with words starting with consecutive letters) or the ever popular (if barely educational) wordsquares, or 'Trackword' out of the *Radio Times*, or whatever. Perhaps you could have a store of ready-duplicated puzzles, for just such emergencies. (Supply teachers will often carry such a store with them.) Games are a bit more risky, unless you are confident with the class. The *Gamesters' Handbooks* have plenty of these (Brandes and Phillips, 1978; Brandes, 1982), but, again, look them up and commit them to memory *before* the emergency crops up.

● Surveys are handy. Get the pupils (who, in emergencies, are often moany) to write down the three things that would improve the school (or the class, or whatever), or the best bits of learning they've done over the last year. Or write a list of all the famous people they have studied – a survey I recommend in the research section of this book as a useful technique for analysing various aspects of learning. Or create a set of rules appropriate for the class, or the school. Or a set of topics that they would like the school council to discuss. Perhaps you could get a group new to the school to write a letter to their previous school, telling them what to expect. Or describe themselves as they expect to be in 10 years. Or write their own obituaries (more fun than you might expect!). I'm sure you can think of more surveys and similar activities. I mention bribery, too. Whatever you set in an emergency, you may want to 'keep things under control' using a bit of bribery – a merit point, or a commendation to the tutor, or whatever the school uses, for the best, quickest, most original, quietist, or fullest contribution.

- Planning for the unplanned includes those scary bits at the end of a lesson, when the pupils are unexpectedly ready to go earlier than you expected, and you have to fill in for 5 minutes. Some teachers use the opportunity to tell the class off for 5 minutes – cruel, I think, but popular with teachers. Some praise the class – which is better but, sadly, harder. Some give a standard talk on the importance of their subject or of education. Some get pupils to describe what they have learned in the lesson (sometimes followed by criticism or praise, *ad lib*). Think of your own.

- Plan for unplanned homework, too, of course. The planned homework may go out the window (for the same reasons the rest of the lesson may go out the window), so what can you set in an emergency? Some of the same puzzles and games can be used (e.g. a Trackword or a letter to a previous school), or you may try setting revision (though you will then have committed yourself to setting a 'test' in the next lesson), or you could pick out any key word relevant to your subject, and get the pupils to ask five adults what that word means to them. A good, all-purpose, well-differentiated, homework, if ever there was one. The word may be a name ('Henry VIII'), or a concept ('betrayal') or a technical term ('pollution'), etc. Think of your own emergency homework, again, relevant to your own subject or interests.

Flexible Learning

'Flexible learning is defined…as the creation of learning opportunities tailored to meet the needs of the learner. Components of this concept include learner autonomy and effectiveness, which are dependent in turn on the extent to which the process of learning is matched to the individual learner's needs for employment or otherwise, via negotiation and counselling and guidance' (FEU, 1983).

It would be particularly inappropriate to be too didactic here about how flexible learning must be organised. Yet we can safely say that promoting flexible learning enables students to be better independent learners, and also enables teachers to be better teachers (differentiating work and giving responsibilities to students), and enables all involved to understand the learning process that much better. Often, a school's librarian will be most expert in flexible learning, yet may not even be consulted by teachers, who too often ignore the skills of non-teaching staff.

'By giving the student increasing responsibility for his or her own learning within a framework of support, teachers will find that, as well as learning the discrete school subjects, students will also develop a range of personal, social, information handling and learning-to-learn skills which considerably enhance personal effectiveness and help contribute to equalise and optimise opportunities for them' (Trayers, in TVEI, 1989).

Teachers often overestimate the variety of the teaching techniques they use, just as they often underestimate the effectiveness of more student-centred techniques. Ask the students (and if you want to know how, look up Black *et al.* 1991).

Every student must be involved in flexible learning. A philosophy of flexible learning would be neutralised if it ignored issues of equality of opportunity, especially with respect to access to resources. I have seen too many resource banks used by groups of students from a narrow range of courses, too many computers used by a narrow range of students, and too many teachers using a narrow range of resources.

'The best teachers are those who choose deliberately and inventively amongst a repertoire of learning activities, or who can judge when the pupils themselves can choose the strategies most likely to advance their learning' (Douglas Barnes, quoted in NCC, 1991).

Group Work

Differentiation can mean wholly individualised learning (as in SMILE Maths), but should also cover various kinds of group work. Ability to take part effectively in group work is, incidentally, also one of the qualities most prized by employers – a fact that is useful to tell pupils. Pupils are often more prepared to say what they do or don't know to each other rather than to you directly. Group work makes use of this willingness to talk to (and help) each other. I am not a great fan of grouping pupils within a class by ability. I'll be convinced that it is useful and effective when I'm prepared, on an INSET day in my own school, for our *staff* to be divided into groups according to the Head's perceptions of *our* abilities. Examples of common groupwork techniques, most of which you'll have used all too often, include:

- *Brainstorming* – Individual, then group pooling, then small groups. For example, 'If you were to have a revolution in the UK in 1994, what would be on your list of things to revolt against? Five minutes to think of your own list, then you'll call them out and I'll write them on the board. Then we'll divide them into different types, and you'll work in groups to agree a final list of revolutionary ideas....'

- *Jigsaw* – Each group learns about one aspect, each reporting back to whole class. For example, 'Each group of you will learn about a character in *Romeo and Juliet*. I want you to agree about why you think they are important, and about what effects you think they have on the plot. In each group, all of you will take part in the discussion, but one should look for events in the play, one should write down what everyone says, and one will report back to the whole group what you've found out.'

- *Two's and four's* – Comparing lists and coming to agreement. For example, 'I want you to categorise these objects according to the materials with which they are made. Working in a pair, write out a list of the categories, and which objects go in which category. After 10 minutes, join another pair, compare your categories, and come to an agreed list – all four of you must agree! Then we'll get the class to see which would be the most useful.'

- *Home-expert-home groupings,* where each initial (home) group learns about one aspect of the topic, then the class is regrouped with just one 'expert' from each initial group in each of the second (expert) groups, reporting their knowledge, with pupils returning at the end of the lesson, perhaps, to the home group to write-up the work. For example (of home-expert grouping, rather than home-expert-home, for a class of 32 pupils): 'Divide into groups of four. Each group will work on one candidate for the crown in 1066. Two groups will investigate William, two Hardrada, two Morcar, and two Harold. I'll give each group member a letter – H, O, M or E. When you've done that, I'll rearrange the groups. There will be two new groups made up entirely of 'H's, two of 'O's, etc. In your new groups, you will have to talk to each other – each member will now be an expert on a different candidate. In your new group, discuss the qualities of the candidates, and fill in the tick list. Then. ...'

- *Ask–talk–record triads* – Where each person, in a set of three, takes a turn at talking about a subject, listening to (or interviewing) the talker, and recording the main points of the conversation. For example, 'You will work in threes on this – one called A, one B, one C. We've studied different types of shops in France. A should pretend to be a French baker, and B should ask them for some bread (or cake); then B should pretend to be a butcher, ..., etc.; then C should pretend to run a post office, ..., etc.'

If you want another incentive to do groupwork, read MacDonald *et al.* (1989). It points out how lack of effective group work can exacerbate racism.

Finally, in this section, how do you assess groupwork? Indeed, do you assess group work? A student teacher I knew got each table-full of pupils at the end of each lesson to come to an agreed mark (from 1 for terrible to 5 for excellent) for how well they've worked as a group. What use could you make of such marks?

DARTs Work

I can remember the first time an inspector asked me whether I used DARTs in the classroom, and I got completely the wrong idea. Since then I've come to appreciate the joys of DARTs (as well as the joys of darts, of course); and whenever I have a text/picture/video, I always (well, usually) think of how I can have *Directed Activities Related to the Text*. It is this idea that helped me to realise how all pupils could have a common experience whilst doing different types and levels of work.

Examples include sequencing, highlighting, matching sections, cloze, re-telling in different format, etc. This allows reasonable access to a very difficult text that might otherwise only be accessible to a few of the pupils. DARTs techniques are at the core of any good use of stimulating resources – whether or not teachers know the term 'DART'.

I like using pictures, especially 'busy' ones, like those of Breughel. What stimulating questions could be used about such pictures – starting with 'What is happening in each of these pictures?' There's a whole book full of pictures, poems, and wonderful ideas for teachers of practically any subject: *Double Vision* by Michael and Peter Benton (1990).

Other interesting 'key' sources which can then be 'DART'ed include maps, videos, artefacts (including videos/pictures of artefacts), songs, or even phrases/quotations (e.g. 'Liberty, Equality, Fraternity'). What good classroom activities, and display work, could you get out of any of these?

Table 7.1 shows an example of a DARTs worksheet on a text from Shakespeare.

Table 7.1 Shakespeare on growing up in early modern Britain

Shakespeare lived from 1564 to 1616. This is what he said about people's lives in the sixteenth century:

As You Like It	*Difficult words*
'All the world's a stage, And all the men and women, merely players; They have their exits and their entrances, And one man in his time plays many parts, His acts being seven ages.	**players** = actors
•	
At first the infant, Mewling, and puking in the nurse's arms:	**infant** = baby **mewling** = crying
•	
Then the whining school-boy with his satchel And shining morning face, creeping like a snail Unwillingly to school.	**whining**=moaning and complaining **satchel** = school bag
•	
And then the lover, Sighing like furnace, with a woeful ballad Made to his mistress' eyebrow.	**furnace** = fire; **woeful** = sad **mistress** = girlfriend
•	
Then, a soldier, Full of strange oaths, and bearded like the pard, Jealous in honour, sudden, and quick in quarrel, Seeking the bubble reputation Even in the cannon's mouth:	**oaths** = swear words **pard** = leopard **bubble reputation** = quick fame
•	
and then, the justice,	**justice** = magistrate or judge

In fair round belly, with good capon lin'd,	**capon** = chicken
With eyes severe, and beard of formal cut,	
Full of wise saws, and modern instances,	**saws** = sayings; **instances** = facts
And so he plays his part.	

•

The sixth age shifts Into the lean and slipper'd pantaloon,	**lean** = thin; **pantaloon** = weak old man
With spectacles on nose, and pouch on side,	**spectacles** = glasses
His youthful hose well sav'd, a world too wide,	**hose** = socks and trousers
For his shrunk shank, and his big manly voice,	**shank** = lower leg
Turning again toward childish treble, pipes,	**treble** = high voice
And whistles in his sound.	

•

Last scene of all, That ends this strange eventful history,	
Is second childishness, and mere oblivion,	**oblivion** = forgetfulness
Sans teeth, sans eyes, sans taste, sans everything.'	**sans** = without

Questions about Shakespeare on growing up in early modern Britain

(1) Which order do Shakespeare's seven ages happen? Put them in the right order.

The lover sighing like furnace	First stage: _____
Second childishness, and mere oblivion	Second stage: _____
The lean and slipper'd pantaloon	Third stage: _____
The justice, in fair round belly	Fourth stage: _____
The infant, mewling, and puking	Fifth stage: _____
The whining school-boy	Sixth stage: _____
A soldier, full of strange oaths	Seventh stage: _____

44

(2) Which bit of Shakespeare's poem do you like best? Write it down here:

_____

_____

_____

(3) Write or draw about each of the seven ages in the 20th Century:

1	2
3	4
5	6
7	

Information Technology in Schools

Technology of every kind, including information technology (IT), has created fear and loathing amongst teachers for years. Some think technology will replace them; some just dislike dealing with potentially unreliable machinery. For the first problem, I would say 'no, but …'. For the second problem, I would say 'fair enough; just make sure you've got alternative lesson plans in case the technology lets you down'.

IT will not replace teachers, but it can make their jobs different. IT nowadays provides far more than just a sophisticated typewriter. CD-ROM systems, with whole encyclopaedias on a single CD, ways of plugging in to a world-wide system of information of all kinds, and developments yet to come, mean that there will be opportunities to change the way we teach. Unsurprising changes include the possibilities that pen, paper, and books could be used less, or that classroom walls will become insignificant learning barriers (i.e. pupils and teachers will no longer have to go *out* and find information). More interesting possible changes will, I think, be the ways in which teaching could become more pupil-centred, with the pupils working (individually or in small groups) on projects or tasks using IT, and teachers acting more like tutors. Flexible learning will become so much easier: it will be difficult to avoid the temptation to move in that direction. Secondary-school teachers have often been reluctant to adopt the good practice of primary-school teachers, including, for example, allowing pupils to take responsibility for many aspects of their progress through the curriculum. Often, the reason given has been that secondary education involves 'imparting' too much specialist information. IT will allow secondary pupils to gain access to information at all levels, and will allow pupils to take part in sophisticated learning schemes that are not immediately teacher led.

Teachers will not become redundant, any more than calculators put all maths teachers out of work, or recorded music put all live musicians out of work. The job changes. (Still scary, perhaps, but a different kind of scary.) Most of the technology is already available that would allow for the kinds of changes envisaged here. What would create the changes would be to do with the politics and economics of education. In the short term, what can or should teachers be looking out for?

- *Use IT as a teacher* – There is a myth that IT speeds work up; it doesn't speed it up, but it does make different kinds of work possible. For example, if you use a lot of work sheets, IT can be used to make them clear and attractive (if you've got the design skills!), and it can be used to make the sheets adaptable – you can edit out the bits that didn't work the first time, or add new bits. Similarly, when doing curriculum plans, these can be adapted and negotiated and revised easily using IT, and a broad curriculum plan can be combined with an individual teacher's lesson plans, to make an effective teaching file. Cross-curricular mapping can also be done relatively easily. Of course, this can all be done with pen and ink; what is useful is to be able to adapt, re-use, and edit quickly. For example, all teachers in a department could combine curriculum plans and lesson plans, and these documents, in turn, could be used to revise the curriculum. Similarly, databases and spreadsheets can make stock control and budgeting more clear and flexible and re-usable, though IT can't make the job 'easy'! Think about what takes you a long time – perhaps record-keeping, planning, writing out class lists, stock checks, or whatever – and see if IT can either make it easier in the short term or at least easier in the long term. Reports on children can be speeded up if you keep a record of what you said last year. The process may be even quicker if you write your own (or plug in to the department's or school's) bank of statements. Simply using word processing, you can create all the commonly used sentences or phrases, and edit these together in interesting and individual ways to create detailed and impressive reports.

- *Use IT with pupils* – Pupils can find great comfort in the neatness of computers (poor or embarrassed writers often seek out computers), in the emotional neutrality of computers (they don't sneer at you or tell you off or use sarcasm), in the social isolation of computers (both an advantage and a disadvantage, of course), or in the opportunities for effective co-operation made available by computers. Pupils may develop greater pride in their work, they may develop a greater sense of their own importance (a word-processed assignment can look so much more significant), they may feel safe enough to try things out – and get things wrong – than they would do without computers. IT should not be something separate from all other activities – either a separate subject alone or a separate section within a subject. It can be a natural part of any lesson. For example, during project work, some pupils may consult and use computers, just as others will be using books or asking teachers. One pupil may be word-processing their work whilst others are writing. One member of each group of pupils might be responsible for searching out information from the computers for the group. A class or departmental 'newsletter' could be produced by editing together pieces of work done on the computer by different pupils through the term. I would counsel against looking for specialist programs to cover every eventuality. The basics of word processing, databases, spreadsheets, drawing, information retrieval using CD-ROMs, and so on, can be imaginatively used within any workscheme.

Homework

A pet topic of mine. Practically every course I've been on has either ignored homework altogether, or, at best, just mentioned it ('Oh, and don't forget how important homework is, either'). With homework, I really do think that we differentiate or die – either differentiate or set mindless tasks or set no homework.

Most schools put a great deal of effort in to getting pupils to do homework, and to getting teachers to set homework. It is used to complement and supplement the classroom experience, to promote strategies of independent learning, to finish off class work, to punish children, to get homes or families involved in education, to research for GCSE coursework, and, no doubt, to fulfil many other functions. However, much less time seems to be spent justifying, planning for, and supporting homework than is spent on class work. There hasn't been so much research on what is done, how it is done, and how homework (like class work) can be planned to meet the needs of different pupils, and allow all pupils equal opportunities to do good work.

Recently (as, intermittently, in the past) there have been some big initiatives on supported study in schools. The Social Services Committee (not the Education Committee) in Strathclyde has funded supported study schemes since 1990 in many of their schools, as an anti-deprivation scheme – trying to break what they saw as a cycle of deprivation, in which pupils in poorer areas were more likely to fail in school because of lack of good learning resources at home. Meanwhile in England and Northern Ireland, the Prince's Trust has worked with LEAs to set up similar schemes. No two schemes, of the dozens currently operating, are alike. Some spend their money on teachers to staff '4–6' clubs for after-school work, some on staff to keep the library open before the start of the school day and at lunch-times; some arrange weekend revision courses; some (like Camden and Belfast) set up study rooms outside the school but close to where many pupils live. There are as many 'schemes' as there are schemes, and many individual schools have run similar projects for years, quite independently of the Strathclyde and Prince's Trust initiatives. What they all have in common is a belief that homework should be treated as a central educational issue, and that once you start one of these schemes, the whole school has an opportunity to address its teaching or homework

strategies, and its relationship to pupils' homes, families or guardians.
A few quotations on homework might be useful:

'While 50% of pupils say that they enjoy school, only 2% say that they enjoy homework' (*TES*, November 1987).

'The success of homework was related to the quality rather than the quantity of the set assignments' (DES, 1987).

'Over the five years of secondary education, appropriate homework can add the equivalent of at least one additional year of full-time education' (Hargreaves, 1984).

'A poor homework policy and/or practice makes its contribution to enlarging the achievement gap between advantaged and disadvantaged pupils' (Hargreaves, 1984).

'A study found that 94% of homework was given at the end of the lesson, half of the time after the bell had rung, and in 9% of cases during the ringing of the bell' (MacBeath and Turner, 1990).

A good exercise would be to work out an ideal, differentiated, weekly 'menu' of homework for a pupil, covering all their subjects, and then compare this to a real menu (by asking the pupils). Other exercises include writing advice to teachers on how to set well-differentiated homework, or advice to pupils on how to organise their homework, or advice to parents or guardians on why homework is important and what they can do to help. (Some of my favourite books on homework are listed in Chapter 14.)

CHAPTER 8

Communication in the Classroom

Introduction

Teaching and learning are done by communicating – mostly by talking, listening, reading and writing. This chapter covers some of the skills used. It starts with listening, partly because teachers and pupils do too little of it: we hear, but we all too seldom listen. After years of teaching, I realised the value of listening only when I went on a counselling course. A teacher who listens effectively can help children express what they didn't realise they knew or felt. Teachers can help pupils, too, with their listening skills.

Talk is a key element in any class, but is rarely credited and rarely assessed. The section on oral work has a quick guide to talking, including 'awkward questions', and looks at some ways of assessing talk. The National Oracy Project and its many training materials take the issue much further.

After a brief section on writing, which is complemented by the work on display and worksheets in Chapter 12, the chapter ends with work on teaching bilingual children. Schools may have few or even no bilingual children, yet the principles described here may help any teacher. All children have to learn the 'language of school', and being sensitive to the ways in which (any) language is learnt can only help a teacher.

Listening

It is inappropriate to give precise guidelines on 'how to listen', but we can try to increase our awareness of different possible listening responses and explain why and how we use them.

An exercise that can help people develop their listening skills is to divide a group into pairs, asking one half of each pair to talk about something interesting (e.g. what they would do if they won £10,000), and the other half to start off listening intently, then gradually lose concentration. Brief the 'talkers' and the 'listeners' separately, of course. In talking about the exercise afterwards, all participants can come up with qualities that make a good or bad listener.

Four common types of verbal listening response can be described:

- A good listener may say something very simple like 'mmm'. These meaningless noises show that we are listening, and help to keep the talking going by encouraging them to say more.

- A good listener will say sympathetic things like 'Oh dear, that's awful...' or 'Yes – do carry on' or 'That's interesting'. These sorts of phrases encourage the talker, showing that we are thinking about them and what they are saying.

- Another type of listening involves questioning – trying to find out what the real meaning is. This 'fishing' may be used to clarify meaning, or encourage a new way of thinking about a topic, or re-direct someone back to the important issue.

- Another response that is particularly helpful is reflecting back to the listener what has been said. For example, Pupil: 'I think King Harold was in a bit of a muddle'. Teacher: 'He was mixed up about what to do next'.

This mirroring can help check the meaning, and can help the talker sort out what is meant. It is also encouraging, and helps stop people 'drying up', when the teacher (or any listener) can't think of anything else to say.

Here is an 'emotional' description of listening (taken from counselling organisations) which teachers and pupils may find interesting:

You are not listening to me when ...

- You do not care about me, and you cannot care about me until you know something about me to care about.

- You say you understand before you know me well enough.

- You have an answer for my problem before I have finished telling you what my difficulty is.

- You cut me off before I have finished speaking.

- You feel critical of my grammar or accent.

- You are communicating to someone else in the room and ignoring me.

- You are dying to tell me something or want to correct me.

- You are trying to sort out all the details and are not aware of the feelings behind the words.

- You sense that my problem is embarrassing and you are avoiding it.

- You need to feel successful.

- You tell me about your experience which makes mine seem unimportant.

You are listening to me when ...

- You really try to understand me when I do not make much sense.

- You grasp my point of view when it goes against your sincere convictions.

- You didn't tell me that funny story you were just bursting to tell me, when I was trying to get help with my work.

- You allowed me the dignity of making my own decisions even though you felt I was wrong.

- You didn't take my problem from me but trusted me to deal with it in my own way.

- You gave me enough room to discover some of my mistakes for myself, and enough time to think for myself what is best.

Talking

Again, there are no fixed rules about talking, but teachers and pupils can be trained to help increase their effectiveness. For teachers, in particular, I would recommend making a tape of a lesson, to analyse the ways in which you and your pupils use their voices. Given a training opportunity, you may find it helpful to develop the technique of asking 'open' questions, i.e. questions that cannot be answered by a simple 'yes' or 'no'. Good talkers may also think carefully about how they sound: intonation. As an exercise, use a list of words (such as gentle, harsh, enthusiastic, bored, sympathetic, tired, angry, welcoming), and work in pairs with one partner, saying 'I'd like to start the lesson now' in the manner of one of the words on the list. The listener must guess how the word was said.

Swap roles and continue with different ways of saying the opening words. Which emotions were easy to express? Which were difficult? Which were easy to misunderstand? Which were obvious?

How do you feel listening to speech which is very loud or very soft? Teachers who shout have little effect except getting a sore throat. If pupils don't listen when you talk softly, they won't listen more if you talk loudly. Try turning your volume down at key moments: you may be suprised how well it works at *increasing* the attention of the pupils.

In face-to-face situations, body language also plays a vital part. Imagine you were on an almost empty bus and a stranger came and sat beside you. You would probably feel threatened – they would be trespassing into what you felt was your territory. However, if the bus was almost full, you probably wouldn't find it threatening – your sense of territory would be modified. If a friend came and sat beside you, it wouldn't matter whether or not the bus was full – you would probably welcome them. But if your mind was dwelling on some complex problem at home or at work, they might be intruding into your sense of privacy and would not be welcome. It is important that we are aware of how our pupils might feel about our body language. Being very close to a pupil can be very threatening; failing to make eye contact when they talk to you may stop them talking, and so on.

Answering Difficult Questions

Pupils are notorious for asking awkward, disturbing or disruptive questions, especially of new teachers. Practise answering some of these, and work out why each one is difficult or annoying. I've included some examples of possible answers. But they are not all that good, and they are certainly not all suited to every teacher!

'How old are you?'

'Let's talk about the work – after all that's the reason we're here.'
'(Why) Is that important (to you)?'
'Getting older by the minute.'
'Old enough to know you should be working.'

'Have you been on holiday?'

'Yes. But I'm back at *work* now!'
'You're interested in holidays. Do you like travelling?'
'Are you good at Geography?'
'Why do you ask? Is it important to know?'

'Can you lend me the bus fare home, I've run out of money?'

'No – sorry – it's our rule.'
'Can you go and get some money anywhere else?'
'How did you run out of money?' (They may be being bullied.)
'What? On the money they pay me to teach you?'

'Have you got a boy/girlfriend?' [And variations, such as 'Are you gay?']

'I won't have any friends at all if we don't get on with this work!'
'I won't ask you about your private life if you don't ask me about mine.'

'Will you be my friend?'

'The school is always here, ready to help you.'

'I'll have a good day at school tomorrow, won't I?'

'I really hope so; it's good to hear you sounding positive.'
'Is that what you're hoping yourself?'
'Why are you worried about the day?'

'Do you want to make me upset?'

'I don't want to at all.'
'No. What is making you upset?'
'What is it makes you most upset?'

'Are you a student?'

(If you are:) 'I've been teaching for years, but I am on a course at the moment, yes.'

'You're not very intelligent, are you?'

'Maybe not, but I'm doing my best.' (See also 'fogging', under bullying.)

'What party (or religion) do you support?'

'I prefer not talking about my politics/religion. It gets in the way of teaching.'

Assessing Oral Work

Oral work of various kinds, including oral assessments (tied in to National Curriculum Attainment Targets and levels), can allow pupils to demonstrate a different range of skills to those demonstrated in written work. Strategic use of oral work can therefore help differentiation a great deal. People have different levels of skill in reading, writing, talking and listening. Good oral/aural work can bring out these different skills. Have you used debates, presentations, question and answer sessions, interviews, role-plays, reading out loud, discussion, making (and listening to) radio or TV shows, spoken tests/quizzes, etc.?

Writing

As well as spoken language, written language will be of concern to teachers. This has also become a political issue in recent years, though it is not always clear exactly what politicians want, other than 'high standards'. The debates over English in the National Curriculum are telling, with reports changed or suppressed, and advice over-ruled. Here are just a few very broad points:

- Skills in writing develop throughout your life. Sometimes secondary-school teachers blame junior-school teachers for not teaching pupils to 'write properly'; sometimes junior-school teachers blame infant-school teachers; infant-school teachers occasionally blame parents. Blame doesn't do anyone much good. Skills can always be improved, and as long as teachers try to do that, i.e. never think it is too late to help pupils with their writing skills. There should be little to blame.

- As with so many areas of education, when it comes to writing, teachers should set a good example. This includes the writing used on boards, but also hand-outs, worksheets and posters. In general, follow the rules you set your pupils. (There is more advice in the section on display, in Chapter 12.)

- Encourage awareness and use of a variety of styles, for different purposes. Examples include newspaper styles (including the special style of headlines), posters and advertisements, dialogue, letter writing, diaries, academic essays, and so on. The 'essay' used to be the standard measure of academic skill, though it has recently become quite rare. (GCSE or A Level students often need a lot of work on essays, as many have previously written few or none.) An unfortunate tendency has been towards writing only single sentences, or even single words, throughout many subjects. This is often done, reasonably enough, to help simplify questions, by breaking them down. However, pupils do need experience of (attempts at) extended writing. They will generally need a lot of support and guidance.

- There are several ways of encouraging effective writing that can raise the profile of the whole issue. For any topic, there are likely to be key concepts related to that topic. A display of these key concepts, with accompanying definitions, can make all pupils more aware of what is distinct about the current topic. Some schools have language diaries – a small booklet in which pupils can write key concepts, or difficult spellings, or interesting words, and in which the school can print its guidance on writing or presentation of work. (In case you think this is 'childish', remember that this book, too, includes lists of key concepts, and definitions of key terms. It is never too late!)

- Individual help given to pupils on their writing is most likely to be through marking books. Regular and effective marking, as I've described in the sections on assessment (Chapter 11) is therefore vital. The school or department may well have guidance on this.

Teaching Bilingual and Multilingual Learners

Many learners in school know more than one language. (In South Camden Community School only 35% of 1992's Year 7 pupils were monolingual English speakers.) The range of languages spoken and written by pupils represents a considerable feat of learning (as many who have attempted, and failed, to become bilingual can testify), and is a great resource for the school. However, if a learner has not yet reached fluency in English in the variety of contexts experienced in school, the school is likely to want to consider how best to support that learner alongside more fluent learners.

The term 'bilingual learner' is generally used to refer to pupils who are not fluent in English and whose first or home language is not English. Technically, this isn't what 'bilingual' means: true bilingualism implies fluency in two languages, not lack of fluency in one! Nevertheless, the term 'bilingual' is used here in the first sense. It should also be noted that many monolingual English speakers (both pupils and teachers) are not fluent in all school contexts.

Whatever definitions of bilingualism and fluency are used, there are strategies that may help when dealing with those at the first three stages of learning English. My descriptions of the stages are adapted from the work of Hilary Hester, and the Camden Language Development Service.

- A Stage 1 learner is new to English; joins in activities with pupils but may not speak; uses non-verbal gestures to indicate meaning; may 'echo' words or phrases of other pupils; etc.

- A Stage 2 learner is becoming familiar with English; growing confidence in using English including holding conversations with peers; more interested in communicating meaning than in 'correctness'; increasing control of English tenses; growing vocabulary of nouns, and beginning to qualify them with adjectives, and using simple adverbs; beginning to write simple stories, but still needs considerable support to operate successfully in written activities.

- A Stage 3 learner is becoming confident as a user of English; great confidence in using English in most social situations; may need support in taking on other registers; developing an understanding of metaphor and pun; increasingly sure of verb system, pronoun system, and sentence structure; pronunciation may be very similar to that of monolingual English speaker.

- Stage 4 refers to bilingual pupils whose use of English and engagement with the curriculum are considered successful and who do not require additional support.

The guidance I'll give was tried on one of my own classes. Of a class of 21 Year 8 pupils, there were two pupils assessed as Stage 1 learners, nine assessed as Stage 2 learners, three assessed as Stage 3 learners, two assessed as Stage 4 learners, and five whose first language was English. The class was able to work successfully on Medieval History, with the help of good planning and a lot of hard work. (Incidentally, this guidance is closely related to all the guidance on differentiation. That isn't really a surprise!)

- *Pupils and their learning activities* – Attitude and motivation, and the learner being relaxed and self-confident, are far more important than, for example, knowing rules of grammar. Learners learn most from their peers and from people with whom they identify. Group work can therefore be vital – two's (e.g. paired reading and completing a chart), four's (e.g. Home-Expert-Home activities, or small role-plays), divided information in large groups, etc. Mix reading, writing, oral and aural work, including in all kinds of assessment procedures DARTs techniques – directed activities related to text. The pupil will first learn current and socially useful phrases. Separate specialist or technical vocabulary can be learnt using a working word list, perhaps on display. Mother tongue practice helps learning of second language.

- *What teachers do* – Explain key words in glossary. Highlight language points as they arise naturally. Use regular patterns, e.g. same phrase used to introduce each activity; same pattern of intro–read–write–talk, etc. Talk about here and now issues, in a natural context, to establish confidence in an immediate context. Reply to the content of what is confidence in an immediate context. Reply to the content of what is said, not its structure (e.g. 'Why are you late?' 'I miss bus' 'Why did you miss the bus?'), and accept non-verbal responses (e.g. a nod) if appropriate. Use concrete referents – food, pictures, toys, etc. – wherever possible. Create an anti-racist and anti-sexist ethos, to make the classroom more relaxed and safe. Allow for a silent phase: don't push, but don't expect this to last for ever (a few weeks or months, in general). Provide a model paragraph. Give visual clues. Every teacher is responsible for language.

- *Learning materials and resources* – Sequencing. Matching starts and ends. Multiple choice sentences, correct sentence to be written out. Provide a sentence table. Use flowchart techniques to assist writing in chronological order. Use picture sequences of process or experiment – match correct text or students provide text. Display should be used both to raise self-esteem and to highlight key points (e.g. health or safety, timelines, experimental techniques, etc.). Display short-, medium- and long-term plans, e.g. blackboard for the day's lesson, temporary display of that half-term's work topic, semi-permanent display of general rules of behaviour, assessment, etc. Display also promotes the use of language itself. Have attractive, readable, resources, using same patterns we expect of children, e.g. underlining titles, capitals only at start of words, etc.

CHAPTER 9

Behaviour in the Classroom

Behaviour is a Learning Issue

The Bad Box
I will put in the box
Bad swearing and rudeness.
I will put in the box
Nasty kicking feet
And bad children, like me.

I will put in
My horrible shouting voice.
My box is made of dark green glass
And you lock it with a key
I will bury it under the ground.

by Lesley Bull (aged 8)

Children often understand behaviour better than their teachers do, and teachers should not forget that. Rather than isolate behaviour, and try to understand it on its own, I've found it useful to look at behaviour problems as *(amongst other things)* curriculum issues. In controlling behaviour, always try to re-direct it towards learning, i.e. never divorce good or bad behaviour from good or bad learning. Effective differentiation can help reduce the misbehaviour caused by academic frustration. Broad issues, such as equal opportunities, can come under this heading, too.

I've included below extracts from an example of a behaviour policy referred to in the Elton Report, and used at Graveney School in Tooting,

South London. I find it useful as a way of focusing on the link between good behaviour and good work. Work within the curriculum that is directly relevant to this might be work on how rules are created (e.g. how the doctrines and practices of Islam are apparently related to the circumstances in which Islam arose), how rules can be re-written (e.g. how the French social system and laws were overturned by the Revolution) and how rules can govern a whole system (as in the laws of physics). Linking rules in the world with rules in the classroom is always useful. 'Bad' behaviour in class can, to a certain extent at least, be put in context for all the pupils. Pupils enjoy making their own rules, and it might be a useful exercise to get them to make a set of school rules 'as if' they were the headteacher, concerned parents, or, indeed, a concerned Secretary of State for Education.

Good differentiation techniques are by their very nature good at encouraging learning and therefore 'good' behaviour. Grouping pupils in different ways, for different (educational) purposes, also, incidentally, splits up 'hard' groups; providing a variety of tasks for all pupils can or should reduce the number of times pupils say 'I'm bored' (although I would hesitate to say there is any way of eliminating this particular remark); etc.

Going back to the pupils' understanding of their behaviour, I should finish by stressing the advantage gained by seeking to know what children believe – through imaginative exercises, but also through their involvement in creating behaviour policies.

Graveney School Behaviour Policy (1990–1991)

'The main aim of the Behaviour Policy is to help create a happy school which fosters good relationships and encourages effective learning.

This Behaviour Policy is based on the principle that all pupils and adults at Graveney are to be valued equally. Adults...includes all those who support pupils at Graveney – schoolkeepers, dinner staff, teachers, office staff, M.R.O., technicians, librarian, nursing staff, cleaning staff, lunchtime supervisors, visiting adults and visiting parents.

The Policy is divided into three sections: relationships, the classroom and the environment. Each section can be summarised by a simple statement.

1   *We should all treat each other with consideration, courtesy and respect*

1.1 We should always show consideration for one another's needs.

1.2 When talking and listening to each other, we should show respect for each other as individuals. Racist and sexist comments, name calling and abusive language are unacceptable.

1.3 Violent behaviour is unacceptable at all times.

1.4 We should treat others as we would wish to be treated ourselves.

1.5 We should show respect for each other's property and that of our community both inside and outside school.

2 *We should make sure that classrooms are places of effective learning*

2.1 Pupils and staff together should take responsibility for creating an enjoyable and productive atmosphere in which learning can flourish. In other words we should make it as easy as possible for pupils to learn and for teachers to teach.

2.2 We should all arrive on time, fully equipped and prepared to start each lesson.

2.3 Homework should be set regularly and completed and handed in on time.

2.4 High standards of attendance and punctuality are expected in order for all to fulfil their potential.

2.5 We should respect others who are learning with us. We should listen to other people when we are asked to do so and follow instructions carefully.

3 *We all have a responsibility to make sure that Graveney is an attractive, safe and healthy environment in which to work*

3.1 Things which are dangerous are not allowed in school.

3.2 We should all move around the school in an orderly fashion, keeping to the left in crowded areas.

3.3 We should all respect, care for and protect our environment and resources.

3.4 We are all expected to be responsible members of the community. We should all take care of the school buildings, classrooms, corridors and toilets and respect and care for the grounds that surround the building. We should only eat in proper places and always put litter in the bins provided.

3.5 Pupils should wear the correct school uniform. Uniform is a means of identification with our school and we are representatives of Graveney wherever we are.'

Bullying in School

What is Bullying?

Of all behaviour issues, bullying is I believe the broadest single problem in school. Kidscape's definition of bullying is 'Repeated intimidation of a victim that is intentionally carried out by a more powerful person or group in order to cause physical and/or emotional hurt'. This may, of course, include racial or sexual abuse or harassment. Causes of bullying, they say, include a permissive attitude towards aggression, an active and quick-tempered temperament, a negative, cold or uninvolved attitude of the primary caretaker, or power assertive child-rearing methods involving physical punishment and violent emotional outburst. Virtually all the information in these sections is adapted from materials produced for Mortimer School, in Streatham, South London, after INSET, discussion and consultation with all teaching staff, the nursery assistant, general attendants and lunch-time supervisors. The Mortimer materials, in turn, made use of the work of Kidscape (e.g. Elliott, 1990), Valerie Besag (1989), and Tattum and Herbert (1990). The examples given of policies and strategies may not be applicable to all schools, but are given as documents from which to work out more suitable materials.

Back in the playground blues – Adrian Mitchell

Dreamed I was back in the playground, I was about four feet high
Yes dreamed I was back in the playground, and standing about four feet high
The playground was three miles long and the playground was five miles wide.

It was broken black tarmac with a high fence all round
Broken black dusty tarmac with a high fence running all round
And it had a special name to it, they called it the Killing Ground.

Got a mother and father, they're a thousand miles away
The Rulers of the Killing Ground are coming out to play
Everyone thinking: who they going to play with today?

You get it for being Jewish

Get it for being black
Get it for being chicken
Get it for fighting back
You get it for being big and fat
Get it for being small
O those who get it get it and get it
For any damn thing at all

Sometimes they take a beetle, tear off its six legs one by one
Beetle on its black back rocking in the lunchtime sun
But a beetle can't beg for mercy, a beetle's not half the fun.

Heard a deep voice talking, it had that iceberg sound;
'It prepares them for Life' – but I have never found
Any place in my life that's worse than The Killing Ground.

How do you Find Out about Bullying?

Every school, of course, is going to have some bullying. Although it is easy to get a false picture of bullying there are many good ways of researching the topic, either within a subject or outside lesson times, appropriate to each school. Confidential questionnaires may work well, if introduced appropriately. Getting pupils to draw maps of safe or unsafe areas in the school seems like a good idea. Pupils at Mortimer School were asked three questions:

What is bullying?
'A bully is a person that always hurts people all the time and says bring things or they would smash your face in or something.'
'A bully is a person who picks on you.'
'A bully is someone who hits me and says rude names.'
'Bullies get you in a corner where the teacher can't see.'
'A bully is when someone hurts you.'

How do bullies make you feel?
'Sad.'
'Terrible.'
'Upset.'
'Scared and frightened.'
'It hurts inside.'
'Bad.'
'Mad.'
'Angry.'
'Sick.'

'Cross, like I want to kill them.'

'Upset, depressed and angry.'

'You start to cry.'

'Horrible.'

'Like punching.'

'Cross.'

What should happen to bullies?

'A bully should get beatings by his mum.'

'They should be put in a children's home.'

'They should be expelled and never come back to school again and no way play with them again if that's the way they are going to treat you.'

'They should be punished severely – like no playing and no trainers.'

'A bully should get bullied by his or her mum and dad.'

Kidscape, in their survey of 4000 children, found that 68% said they had been bullied, 38% said they had been bullied more than once, and 12% had been severely bullied, with effects such as attempted suicide, repeatedly running away from home, self-mutilation, and/or truancy.

Tackling the problem as a whole school – Extracts from a Bullying Policy

The school is a community where each member should be responsible for himself or herself and for the well-being of all others. The aim of a bullying policy is to help achieve this sense of community by involving all pupils and adults in the prevention of bullying. We also aim to help all pupils feel safe in the knowledge that there are clear rules backed by appropriate systems to protect and support victims.

Parents of current and new pupils will receive details of the policy. New pupils will be given information, appropriate to their age and understanding, when they are admitted to the school. Existing pupils will be given an introduction to the policy during school assembly and in tutorial periods. They will be reminded of the policy during the first tutorial period after each school holiday. Details of the policy will naturally be reinforced by the staff if incidents of bullying occur. A notice about the bullying policy will be displayed in each classroom. A copy of this policy will be included in the Staff Handbook. Governors will also be given copies of the policy.

The staff, of course, have to be committed to the policy too. All members of staff are expected to examine their own behaviour and to set a good example at all times. To prevent opportunities for bullying, staff must also examine the school's physical environment and general organisation and be alert to possible 'danger' areas. Pupils must be well supervised at all times. All members of staff should be alert and should intervene whenever they observe any incidents of name-calling, etc. The everyday racist and sexist language and actions of many pupils and adults must always be tackled.

The curriculum can tackle bullying in various ways. Teachers will aim to create a caring co-operative ethos. In addition to teaching social behaviour by drawing on incidents as they occur in the daily life of the class, teachers and ancillary staff must play an important role in teaching social skills in a conscious and systematic way. The PSE programme will contain specific sections on bullying. Opportunities should be provided for groups to discuss bullying in role-playing situations devised to help pupils cope better with bullies. Similarly, bullies should be placed in situations which require them to see things from the victim's perspective.

These, and similar, activities may take place in PSE, English, and other lessons, and it will sometimes be appropriate for Assemblies to examine themes related to bullying. Many pupils would also benefit from a course of assertiveness training (including techniques such as 'broken record', 'fogging', and practising saying 'no') as an alternative to passivity or aggression. There must be discussion amongst staff to ensure that similar standards are enforced by all.

Dealing with Victims

When a pupil reports that he or she has been bullied, the member of staff should take the following action:

- Praise the pupil for reporting the incident.

- Respond with sympathy and take the report seriously.

- Give the pupil time to voice her or his feelings.

- Explain to the victim what will happen to the bully.

- (Later) Report the incident to the victim's tutor.

As a result of previous negative experiences, some pupils may become chronic victims. These pupils need extra, long-term support. This support should include:

- Helping the pupil recognise and eliminate any provocative behaviour.

- Teaching appropriate responses.

- Giving advice about self-protection.

Children who become chronic victims usually do so as a result of their low self-esteem. Therefore, we must also take positive steps to build self-esteem. In order to do this we must:

- Aim to meet the pupil's needs through the curriculum so the pupil feels a sense of achievement.

- Provide activities designed to improve social skills.

- Praise and reward effort, achievement and appropriate behaviour.

Dealing with Bullies

Pupils must understand, and believe, that bullying will not be tolerated. This can be achieved only if all incidents are dealt with firmly. When dealing with a pupil who has bullied, the member of staff should take the following action:

- Confront the pupil with the incident.

- Make sure the pupil understands why his or her actions were considered to be bullying.

- Help the pupil to consider the feelings of the victim.

- Help the pupil to consider suitable reparation.

- Ensure that this reparation is carried out.

- (Later) Report the incident to the bully's tutor, put note in the file, etc.

As a result of previous negative experiences, some pupils may become chronic bullies. If the pupil continues to bully, we will take the following action:

- Staff should carefully log details of the bullying.

- The pupil's tutor should inform the Deputy Head, who will write to the pupil's parents or carers inviting them to come to a meeting at school.

- The Deputy Head (in discussion with the pupil's tutors) will prepare a Home/School contract to be discussed with the pupil and parents or carers at the meeting.

The Home/School Contract should make explicit:

- What is expected of the pupil.

- What the school will do to support the pupil.

- How parents or carers can support the pupil.

- What sanctions will be used if the bullying continues.

- Method of liaison with home.

- How, and when, the contract should be reviewed.

The contract should be signed by the pupil, the parents or carers, and a representative of the school. Extracts from an example are printed below. If there is an improvement in the behaviour, it is important to recognise this and praise the pupil. If the pupil continues to bully, the sanctions stated in the contract will have to be used. Parents or carers will be informed of the outcome. If the bullying continues, despite sanctions, the matter may be referred to the Headteacher with a view to excluding the pupil from school. A new contract should be negotiated with the Headteacher, Deputy Headteacher, and parents or carers at the meeting which takes place when a pupil returns from a period of exclusion. If the bullying still persists, the matter should be referred to the school Governors for advice about further action.

Children who become chronic bullies usually do so as a result of their low self-esteem. It is therefore essential that we also take positive steps to build self-esteem. In order to do this we must:

- Aim to meet the pupil's needs through the curriculum so the pupil feels a sense of achievement.

- Provide activities designed to improve social skills.

- Praise and reward effort, achievement and appropriate behaviour.

What do we say to pupils? Extracts from Advice to Pupils

Bullies are people who use their powers over and over again to hurt or upset other people. Bullies can make life miserable for other children. Some people are bullies because they are unhappy or insecure, bullied at home, unhappy with themselves, not allowed to show their feelings, or cowards at heart. Bullies can seem very powerful. They may even make it look as if the bullying is the victim's fault.

Why is it important to stop bullying? Our School is a community. Everyone needs to look after themselves and each other. Stopping bullying will help everybody – the victims, the bullies and the whole school. It is everyone's responsibility to take an active part in stopping bullying.

What should you do if someone bullies you or if you see someone bullying another person? Report bullying to an adult. You can tell any teacher, or anyone else who works in the school. If you want to speak to someone in private, you can go to see [teacher] at these times...

What will happen when you report bullying? All members of staff have agreed that it is essential to prevent bullying. Someone will deal with the bully as soon as possible. The staff will get together to decide what punishment might be suitable.

What if a pupil does not stop bullying? If this happens, the school will send for the pupil's parents to come to a meeting. The pupil will have to sign a special contract. If this does not help, we may have to exclude the pupil from school. This would be a very serious matter.

Some things to do if you are being bullied:

- Tell an adult you trust.

- Tell yourself that you don't deserve to be bullied.

- Get your friends together to say no to the bully.

- Stay with groups of people, even if they are not your friends. There is safety in numbers.

- Try to ignore the bullying.

- Try not to show you are upset, which is difficult.

- If possible, avoid being alone in places where bullying happens.

- Walk quickly and confidently even if you don't feel that way inside. Practise!

- If you are in danger, get away. Do not fight to keep possessions.

- Fighting back may make it worse. If you decide to fight back, talk to an adult first.

- If you are different in some way, be proud of it! It is good to be an individual.

Extracts from a Contract for a 10-Year-Old Bully

Why are we holding this meeting? People at this school are all very worried about X bullying other children. We want to help him change three things. The first is the way X sometimes hurts other children. The second is the way he frightens them by threatening to hurt them. The third is the way he orders them about and makes them do what he wants. Why is it important to change things? There are two important reasons why we will not allow X to go on behaving in this way. First, all children have the right to feel safe, secure and happy at school. It is not fair for them to be frightened by bullies. Second, we want X to do well. It is important for his future happiness that X learns how to behave with other people.

These are our rules for X: X should do his best to make sure that children in his company do not have to worry about being hurt by him. X should do his best to make sure that children in his company do not feel threatened by him. X must allow people to make their own choices and decisions.

This is how we will help X: We will give X as much support and encouragement as possible. We will, of course, deal with anyone who bullies X. How will we know when X's behaviour improves? The Deputy Head will tell all members of staff to watch X carefully and to write in a special diary if there are any incidents of bullying. We will send a copy of the diary home so they know what is happening. What will happen when X's behaviour improves? We will keep in close contact with home so everyone can praise X's progress. We will speak with home to agree on a reward when he shows us an improvement in his behaviour.

What will happen if there is no improvement? X must stop bullying. If he does not make a very good effort to improve we will have to deal with his behaviour very seriously. We might have to remove X from the playground at break time and lunch-time. We might have to say he must sit with a teacher in the dining-room at meal times. We will keep in close contact with home and arrange for X to miss something he likes at home. If this does not help then we would have to speak to the school governors to see if they think X should stay at this school.

Please sign below to state that you understand and agree with these rules.

Bullying in the Curriculum

Here are some ideas for teachers, expanding on suggestions made earlier in this guide. I've categorised them under subject headings, but I realise that practically any of the activities could come up in practically any of the school subjects.

PSE: There are specialist guides available to assertiveness training, but aspects of assertiveness can easily be taught by any interested teachers, especially if they take PSE lessons. Being assertive definitely does not mean being aggressive: an assertive person deals with situations maturely – and aggression is very unlikely ever to be a mature response. Being assertive is roughly equivalent to being 'adult', as described in Transactional Analysis, with aggression usually being like a 'parent'. Here are three handy, assertive, responses to other people's aggression (i.e. bullying). 'Broken record' involves repeating over and over again (like a broken record) a short phrase, saying what you want. This should be done in a calm but clear voice. Phrases might be 'I don't think it's right to steal, so I won't do it', 'I don't want to fight you', 'Let's sit down and discuss this calmly' (a good one for teachers to use!), or whatever. The important thing is not to get side-tracked, and not to get louder and louder. This technique can work well with exceptionally aggressive people. A simple, calm, phrase, if repeated often enough, can be the only thing that will 'get through' to someone who's really wound up. Staff working in casualty departments are often trained to use the technique, so watch out for it on *Casualty*. 'Fogging' involves 'swallowing up' an insult (like a fog), so that it loses its effect. Surprisingly, it usually involves agreeing with the insult. For example, you could reply to 'You're stupid' with 'Maybe I am, but I at least I try my best' ; 'This is boring' with 'I'm sorry if you find it boring, but we still have to do it' (good for teachers!); 'You're a fat ugly git' with 'Yes, but at least I've got better manners than you have'. The general rule is, agree with the insult if you think it is true, admit the possible truth if it might be true (e.g. 'Perhaps, but...'), and acknowledge the insult (e.g. 'I know that's what you think, but...') if you think it is false. The third common technique to help improve assertiveness is simply to practise saying 'No!', clearly and loudly. This can be an especially rewarding task if you can separate out the normally quiet members of the class (in many schools, the girls) and get them to practise on their own.

History: There is plenty of bullying in history, and when topics arise naturally in your teaching, it is worth bringing out the issue of bullying. It may be that pupils find it easier, safer, and even more enlightening discussing Henry VIII's cruelty to his wives, or Nazi persecution of practically everyone, or William the Conqueror's suppression of the Anglo-Saxons, than their own experiences of bullying, or family or social cruelty.

English: Easy. I recommend the opening section of Maya Angelou's *I Know Why the Caged Bird Sings* (1969) – a wonderful book for adults, too, who want to understand.

Maths: Use imagination. The map work mentioned earlier, calculating how often bullying takes place in different parts of the school, for example, can easily become a maths project.

Technology: Design a bully-free school?

Art: Paint your own nightmares? Dreams are often the way pupils best describe bullying. Dream analysis may also be done, sensitively, in PSE. (Ann Faraday's book *Dream Power* (1972) is excellent, and has a section on using dreams in school.)

Music: You could do well setting the Adrian Mitchell poem to music. It's written in the style of lyrics to a standard 12-bar blues – the sort that are supposed to start 'I woke up this mornin'...'. It's probably too risky to use the otherwise interesting 'Tubby the Tuba' as it may stimulate name-calling.

Please think of your own ideas, too, relevant to the subjects you expect to teach, and ideas for form-, year-, or whole-school assemblies. The single most useful strategy I've used involves getting a 'victim' to think about whether they would rather be themselves or the bully. I've not come across a victim who would prefer to be the bully. This strategy is similarly useful for teachers who feel or are victimised by pupils or other staff. There is much strength to be drawn from realising you would rather be you.

CHAPTER 10

Cross-Curricular Controversial Issues

Controversy in the Curriculum

Controversial issues come up in school, whether you like it or not. Teaching itself is controversial – both in the basic sense that people disagree over the value and role of teaching and in the sense that there are inevitably conflicts and contradictions within every class and every subject that you teach. Teachers who think that there is no conflict in their classes (perhaps because there is no visible conflict), or who think that ignoring controversial issues is the best way of dealing with them, will be failing their pupils. The opposite problem is of teachers thinking that society is so split by conflicts and disagreements that they expect and allow all kinds of divisions to spill into the classroom. The classroom should be an island of calmness, maturity and mutual care, but it can only be such an island if it recognises the stormy seas surrounding it, out of which come all the school's pupils and staff.

As I wrote in the section on ethics (above, Chapter 3), teachers 'shouldn't arbitrarily try to impose their own convictions on schools concerning politics, philosophy or religion' and that 'if we talk about our beliefs, even if they are the same as those of the pupils, we have started imposing our views, however gently we express them'. That is my starting point. There are many individual controversial issues that could be covered in this section. You probably have expert knowledge on controversies that are particular to your school or part of the country, or to your subject, or of which you have personal experience. Many controversial issues are sidelined in schools. Some appear in the sections of the National Curriculum called 'cross-curricular themes', others simply appear in the classroom, at any time, and so, too, can be called 'cross curricular'.

PSE and Tutoring

PSE (Personal and Social Education) and tutoring appear to be the main bearers of cross-curricular themes in today's schools. There is no legally compulsory subject called PSE, although almost all schools will have such a subject. It may be called PSE, or PSHE ('health'), or PHSE, or PSME ('moral'), or tutor period, or ATW (Active Tutorial Work), etc.

The Education Reform Act (1988) says that the aims of schooling include to 'promote the spiritual, moral, cultural, mental and physical development of pupils at the school and of society', and to 'prepare…pupils for the opportunities, responsibilities and experiences of adult life'. This is inevitably done in many areas of a school's life, but may be focused on in PSE lessons, or in the role of the tutor. The National Curriculum talks of the cross-curricular skills as including 'personal and social' skills, and cross-curricular themes include economic and industrial awareness, careers education and guidance, health education, education for citizenship, and environmental education. Again, these may be done anywhere in the school, but many schools use PSE or tutoring to cover (some would say 'mop up') much of the work.

Tutoring does generally include some very specific tasks, legally formulated in the 1987 Conditions of Employment for Teachers (which apply to virtually every teaching job in the state sector). These include: 'Promoting the general progress and well-being of individual pupils and of any class or group of pupils assigned to him [or her].' 'Providing guidance and advice to pupils on educational and social matters and on their further education and future careers including information about sources of more expert advice on specific questions; making relevant records and reports.' 'Making records of and reports on personal and social needs of pupils.' 'Communicating and consulting with the parents of pupils.' 'Communicating and cooperating with persons or bodies outside the school.' 'Participating in meetings arranged for any of the purposes described above.' 'Registering the attendance of pupils.'

The theory of PSE and tutoring has been well described by Chris Watkins and NAPCE (the National Association of Pastoral Care in Education). They talk about the pupil as a whole human being, who can be thought of as having a bodily self, a sexual self, a social self, a vocational self, a moral self, a self as a learner, and a self in the organisation. You should be able to work out the significance and meaning of all of these selves.

Michael Marland (e.g. in Marland, 1989) and others write about different styles of tutoring. In some schools, the tutor has a very central role, with access to all information, always consulted by other staff, always present at interviews with parents, etc. In some schools, information is mostly available to tutors on request, who are kept informed of actions by senior staff, etc. Tutors in other schools don't get confidential information, and are generally bypassed, simply filling in the register and doing other routine administration. The first of these systems is the most fashionable – and therefore worth thinking about if you get a job interview.

John Miller (1982) usefully describes the typical work of a tutor – with his book concentrating on FE tutoring – as involving the following tactics:

- *Taking action* – Referring on, telling someone, writing a letter, etc.

- *Advising* – Describing strategies or alternatives (not 'If I were you...').

- *Changing the system* – Acting on the fact that the problem may be one of the school.

- *Teaching* – Introducing new thoughts and ideas, making sense of the pupil's world (not didactic).

- *Informing* – Introducing sources of information.

- *Counselling* – Giving the pupil an opportunity to talk through a problem.

  (Giving 'TACTIC'.)

In practice, PSE and tutoring are sometimes combined, and are done by the same person. Sometimes PSE is taught by specialists in a department of their own. Sometimes tutoring and PSE are both seen as minimal activities (e.g. registering, and signing homework diaries), with the key bits taught within other subjects (for example, sex in Science, environment in Geography, morals in RE, counselling by a Counsellor, etc.). Sometimes the whole lot seems to be done by the (poor, beleaguered) tutor. One of the key issues can be the status of the tutor or PSE teacher – their status in the eyes of the school (as Marland describes) and their status in the eyes of the pupils. If PSE or tutoring has a low status, then, whatever the theory, the practice (and the practitioner) is likely to suffer!

I've heard schools tell new teachers 'PSE is as good as you make it'. This attitude sums up one of the problems of PSE, but it also highlights the opportunity you may well be given to teach subjects, and use teaching strategies, which are exciting and relevant.

During the PGCE year, students should try to teach some PSE, either as a 'regular' part of their teaching practice, or as an extra (perhaps team teaching with the tutor, or with another student), or even in another school or outside their teaching practice. I have on several occasions recommended using PSE lessons, for example, as a source of data for research. For example, someone studying bullying might try to teach a series of lessons on the topic; someone studying methods of writing annual reports might 'consumer test' different styles of reports on pupils in a PSE lesson. Remember, of course, to seek appropriate permission. Mind you, I've rarely heard a teacher refuse an offer to 'donate' a PSE lesson to a willing volunteer.

Sex and Health Education

Of all the issues covered by the broad heading 'personal and social', it is teaching about sex and health that seem to cause most worries amongst teachers. This is neither surprising nor unreasonable: teachers are used to being, or being treated as, 'experts', yet when it comes to sex and health, there's no evidence of teachers being, or being seen as, particularly expert. Some schools solve this by bringing in 'experts'. Others are happy to challenge the view of teachers as experts by encouraging, for example, peer tutoring. Whatever is done, teachers are likely to need good, sensitive, training, and the school must anyway have a policy on sex education. All teachers should avoid hurting, upsetting or embarrassing pupils by how they deal with these issues. This can be done all too easily, by making assumptions about pupils (e.g. about boyfriends or girlfriends) or by treating issues as trivial that are important to pupils.

On the issue of sex, remember that of a class of 30 pupils, all will have thought about sex, many will have had (pleasant and/or unpleasant) sexual experiences, many will be uncertain about their sexuality, some will be homosexual or lesbian, all will have been given different (correct and incorrect) information by different people, almost all will feel guilty about some aspect of sex, most will think everyone else knows (or has experienced) more than they do.

On the issue of health, remember that of a class of 30 pupils, all will have had a wide experience of both health and illness, with an average of one in 30 school children having suffered the loss through death of a close member of their family. (Death and loss are issues that could appropriately be seen as a separate controversial issue.) It is too easy for teachers to think that telling pupils of health dangers is enough to stop them taking risks. This is, sadly, rubbish – as teachers should know just by looking around the staffroom at the (perfectly intelligent) teachers who smoke or drink or take no exercise or whatever. What is needed is an engagement with the information. Pupils must *want* to be healthier.

Teachers may appropriately tackle many of these issues in specialist academic subjects as well as in PSE and tutor time. (The issues can of course come up at any time, and often arise through insults based on sex or sexuality or on illness or disability.) I enjoy books on disease and History or creativity (e.g. Cartwright, 1972; Sandblom, 1982), but then that may say more about me than it does about the topics!

HIV/AIDS brings together sex and health issues, of course, and is a good example of a controversial issue that can't be avoided. One of the early public health campaigns ended with the tag 'don't die of ignorance'. Whether or not such scare-mongering is the best way to tackle HIV/AIDS, it is certainly a good way of getting teachers to realise that they shouldn't avoid controversial issues.

Politics

Politics covers national and international issues, but also internal school issues. It is a matter of power (who has it, and with what legitimacy), of rights and duties (and their implementation), and of change (progressive or regressive) and conservation (in its broadest sense). The larger-scale issues may come in particular syllabuses (for example in History or in PSE), or may be brought out in special events (such as mock elections at the time of a local or national election). 'Citizenship' is the name most often given by recent governments to political education, and this often stresses those large-scale issues. Pupils tend to be more sensitive, though, to smaller-scale issues: the rights or duties of people within the school, pupil involvement in decision-making, or the fairness (justice) with which issues or people are dealt. This is also a proper concern of citizenship education. It is no good having teachers extol the virtues of democracy whilst demonstrating dictatorship. (It would be equally bad to *pretend* to have a democratic school whilst being unable to run it that way!) School councils often play a big role in this side of the school. I will mention, in this section on politics, the related issues of environmental education (currently a big political issue in every sense), and economic and industrial awareness (and careers education), which can properly be dealt with in similar ways, but which I will not cover in detail.

Racism and Sexism

At the age of 4, white British children are likely to exhibit quite sophisticated forms of racism, not only having negative views of other races, but also understanding that these views should not be expressed to certain adults (see Carrington and Troyna, 1988). If this is true of children at 4, imagine how much more sophisticated forms of racism may be exhibited by older children. Two popular myths: 'There's no racism (or sexism) in this school' and 'Racism (or sexism) isn't a problem in this school because it is all white (or single sex)'. We don't get rid of prejudice against a group by getting rid of the group – if it worked like that, Hitler would have cured Germany of anti-Semitism.

There are two stages in tackling racism and sexism. The first is the recognition stage. Pupils, like staff, must recognise the existence of various groups in society. It may seem obvious, but plenty of textbooks mention no or very few women, and have no portrayals of people from ethnic or racial minority groups. This stage also involves recognising that there is prejudice and discrimination. There is no easy way to tackle the comment (all too common amongst pupils and teachers) that there is no such thing as racism or sexism, only black people or women 'with chips on their shoulders'. Sensitive use of literature and television programmes is likely to be more effective than simply dismissing such remarks as foolish.

The second stage in tackling racism and sexism is trying to reduce it. This of course involves making a moral judgement (which shouldn't be hidden) – that racism and sexism should be reduced. Most if not all schools, and all LEAs, in common with governments (of all the major parties), have policies opposed to racism and sexism. This is the excuse (if excuse is needed) for being so bold and moral. However, just because you are making a moral judgement, it doesn't mean that you need to be hurtful or unpleasant to racists or sexists. It is hardly likely to cure people of prejudice if they are made to feel stupid or hated.

Religion and Worship

It can be very difficult understanding views on religion that differ from your own, particularly if you have religious beliefs founded on faith and not subject to rational doubt. Birthdays may not seem controversial, but some religions regard celebrating birthdays as wrong. Drawing a picture of a person may not seem controversial, but some religions may not allow the depiction of living things. Referring to 'Jesus Christ' ignores the controversy (most obviously between Christians and Jews) over whether Jesus really was the Christ (Jews believe the 'Messiah', the Hebrew word for 'Christ', is yet to come). Teaching Darwinist versions of evolution may offend religious groups. Problems arise not only because it is easy to offend people, but because some religious beliefs may conflict with practices or beliefs built in to the school. Some problems may be solved without too much difficulty: biologists may replace dissection of real animals with models; Christmas services may be replaced with end-of-term shows; uniform regulations may allow girls to wear trousers or may allow turbans to replace caps; and so on. Harder to deal with are problems such as the racism or sexism which many religions (or many interpretations of many religions) may exhibit, which may conflict with strongly held school policies. Similarly difficult is the legal requirement to begin every school day with an act of worship 'concerned with reverence or veneration paid to a divine being or power' (DFE, 1994a) which pupils have no right to opt out of, may conflict with a school's beliefs about freedom of conscience. (It is parents or guardians, *not* pupils, who can take children out of acts of worship.) Many schools solve this last difficulty by not having an act of worship. (This creates another possible problem, of justifying breaking the law!)

Religion is inevitably controversial, then. Difficulties can't be solved by a simple policy of 'tolerance', as tolerance of religious beliefs may bring with it tolerance of racism or sexism or lawbreaking or intolerance of non-believers. As with other controversial issues, it is important to separate the issue from the person, and avoid being hurtful or cruel to someone because of their religious beliefs (or because of their doubts or their atheism), even if you do not allow them to practise what they believe in school. Schools with religious foundations will of course solve many problems by being explicitly Catholic or Church of England or Jewish, etc., and these schools are also likely to see religious issues as important enough to debate and have policies on. Such schools will not, however, solve all problems, any more than a church itself can avoid controversy.

CHAPTER 11

Assessment and Evaluation

Purposes and Strategies

Why Assess?

The only way to make the conversion from an 'expert', who knows a lot, to a 'teacher', who helps people learn, is by understanding what your audience already knows and how they learn. Assessment includes the learning that every teacher does. You learn about your pupils from the moment you walk into the room – you learn how they react, how to get them to do things, how to pitch your talking or writing so they understand, and so on. There are three specific purposes of assessment that I'd like to highlight:

- Assessment, especially more formalised assessment (like marking), is the clearest way to understand more about individual pupils: what stimulates them (see 'Equal Opportunities'), what needs they have (see 'Special Educational Needs'), and so on.

- Good quality assessment is the main method you have of finding out how to differentiate your work, i.e. if you are going to set appropriate tasks for your pupils, you need to be constantly finding out what they know or can do. Well-organised, differentiated, learning is founded on good assessment.

- The assessment process itself is often, surprisingly, the most personal, 'intimate', side of your relationship with individual pupils. In your everyday marking, you are having a private conversation with each pupil, and you can build up a relationship with their work that is all but impossible in the managed chaos of the classroom. In your longer term assessments (perhaps for reports or parents' evenings, or for National Curriculum records) you can help stimulate change and progress that you might not even envisage in your work in the classroom. You can involve pupils in their own learning, by having self-assessment (and course-assessment) tasks. You will find, incidentally, that pupils tend to be much more harsh and critical about themselves than you would ever be – a reflection, often, of their low self-esteem, and/or their perceptions, realistic or not, of what you and their other teachers think of them.

What Strategies Should be Used?

Think about what works best for you. In other words, how would you like to be assessed? What about specific strategies? Here goes:

- *Having clear criteria is important* – Don't say 'this piece of work isn't long enough' if you haven't said how long it should be. Tell the pupils what your criteria are, and change the criteria to suit the occasion – for example, 'neatness' might be a vital criterion in assessing display work, but less vital in assessing notes on a television programme. (Having clear criteria links with being fair.)

- *Being positive is important* – Especially, being positive first, before any less positive comments. For example, 'You've worked hard on this research, Yarnell, and I really like your picture of Queen Elizabeth. Could you remember to underline your titles?' is, I think, better than 'Could you remember to underline your titles, Yarnell? You've worked hard on this research, and I really like your picture of Queen Elizabeth.' Pupils generally react most (whether favourably or unfavourably) to the first comment they read.

- *Give unqualified praise, where it is due* – Never 'but'. 'A great piece of research, Angela' is better than 'A great piece of work, Angela – but why couldn't you always work like this?'. (The word 'but' denies the phrase it follows – as you may recognise in the phrase 'I really love you but...'.)

- *Being fair is important* – Don't knock marks off for bad behaviour, unless the assessment is about behaviour. Don't give two people different marks or comments for the same level of work just because one pupil gets on your nerves. (Studies have suggested that even experienced exam markers do respond to simple and irrelevant things, like the examinee's name, in giving marks.)

- *Most important of all is speed* – Assessment should have an effect on future work. The effect is inversely proportional to the time gap between work and assessment. If you can't get work (especially homework) marked and handed back by the next lesson (or within a week in the case of work done quite separately from the normal work, like a test) then you are probably only assessing for your benefit. There is unlikely to be any effect on the pupil. If you teach five classes, then, you should aim to do (at least) five sets of marking a week. If this seems to take too long, then just speed up your marking. If it still seems to take too long, then complain to the Government about your conditions of service, or cut down on the other things you do, or moan. Don't take it out on the pupils!

Formal Testing or Exams

Most teachers, virtually all secondary teachers, will be involved in public exams; most, again, will administer school tests of some kind, too.

Public Exams

- If you teach to a public exam, get the syllabus. It may sound obvious, but many teachers rely on their memory of the syllabus, or on a departmental summary of a syllabus. Get the original. (Not always that easy, or cheap. If the school can't help, try the exam boards or the public library.) Get all the past exam papers while you're at it. It is a good idea to give the syllabus, or edited highlights of it, and past exam papers, to the pupils – perhaps make a display of them – so the pupils know (and can feel responsible for) what's expected, too.

- Teach to the syllabus and any exam papers available (which may have different emphases). There's no excuse for spending a lot of time doing things that won't help the pupils get through the exam. I wouldn't suggest being boring: a syllabus may itself be boring, but its content should be inspiring!

- Teach in such a way that a pupil in your class could get a top grade. This is particularly important if you have a class that is very challenging, or in which you expect few high grades. Allow for excellence. (Of course, strive for excellence and encourage it at all times. But always remember *at least* to allow for it!) This may mean setting flexible tasks, giving alternative homework, and so on, so that the pupils have a sense of choice or opportunity.

- Teach in such a way that a pupil in your class could successfully complete the course, fail the exam, and still have had a worthwhile educational experience. Sadly, pupils fail. The least we can do is give a failing pupil a good education. The education should be worthwhile in its own right. We should avoid teaching in such a way that prospective failures are sidelined or ignored, or have nothing to do. (We should be happy to answer the question, seriously asked of a GCSE English teacher getting the pupils to write their name and course on their folders, 'How do you do a 'G', sir?'.)

- Where there are coursework requirements, remember that obedience is as valuable as intelligence. What I mean is that a considerable number of pupils gain lower grades than they might expect because they don't follow the instructions. This is as true of the post-graduate students I've taught as any 15-year-old GCSE student. Meet deadlines; do cover pages; put titles on graphs; do 3,000 to 5,000 words. Or whatever the syllabus says.

- Results can hurt. Teach in such a way that you can at least say to yourself 'well, I did my best'. An interesting way to analyse the results of the pupils you have taught is to look at their other grades and see if they got a higher or lower grade for you than for their other subjects. This is quite a sensitive indicator of your success compared with your colleagues, although there are always other factors at work. Schools may have their own systems of analysis. Remember that if you get a poor set of results one year, it should at least be easy to improve next year.

- If you get a chance, apply to be an exam marker. It is a terrible, stressful, underpaid, job, that can ruin the Summer term for you. However, you will also learn more about how to teach to exams than you possibly thought you could.

School Exams

- Schools, or departments, or individual class teachers, may set exams. If they do, try to get involved in the process. Setting exams is a valuable experience, and much harder than you might expect.

- Differentiation is the key to setting good exams. There should be something for everyone to do, for the whole period of the exam. (This is a matter of behaviour management as well as self-esteem and encouraging learning at all levels. You don't want to have to entertain or control some pupils whilst others finish an exam.) Incorporate tasks that can have a lot of time taken over them by pupils who may not understand, or may not have revised for, many questions; incorporate tasks that can have a lot of time taken over them by pupils who can complete most questions very quickly. I have recently taken to adding a last question saying something like, 'Now, write down or draw anything else you know about this topic'. A bit of a cheat, I know, but handy for all sorts of reasons.

- Exams test exam technique as well as subject skills or knowledge. You can separate the two measures, to a certain extent, by having a variety of types of questions or tasks. Some might rely on memory, some on skill, some on powers of logic. Or whatever. You may want a mixture of, say, multiple choice questions, extended writing, matching starts and ends of sentences, repeating or copying exercises, demonstrating understanding of texts, and so on.

- Whether or not you teach English or another language, all exams are likely to be tests of language. Try to make sure that the language of exams is no more complex than it need be. Many exams are better at sorting out pupils according to their language skills than their skills in the nominal subject of the exam. As a rule, keep sentences short. Say no more than one thing in each sentence. For example, it is better to split 'examine the causes and effects of the French Revolution' into two questions. Use as few qualifying phrases as possible. For example, avoid a question like 'In your own view, given the evidence in items A to C, what do you think is the most important of the many causes of the French Revolution?'; convert it, at least, to 'Use the evidence in A to C. What is the most important cause of the French Revolution?'. Computers these days can check the 'readability' of text. This book, for example, is measured by my computer as requiring the reading skills of an average American in grade 12, and would be readable by 69% of Americans. (That'll teach me to buy American software.) Too high, in other words, for most school children.

- Mark exams quickly. One of the tests of a good exam is that there is a spread of marks, and that, if percentages are given, no one scores 0% or 100%. All internal exams should be seen (at least partially) as 'formative' assessments: as something to work on for the future.

Marking and Reporting in Practice

There are two more things to be done on assessment and evaluation:

- *How have you (and how could you have) turned theory into practice?*
  What systems of weekly record-keeping have you been doing? What
  are the advantages and disadvantages of your system? Think about
  time, effort, clarity, usefulness for the department or school, usefulness
  for lesson planning, monitoring homework, covering the National
  Curriculum, identifying special needs, etc. What systems of yearly (or
  perhaps termly) reporting are used in the school? How useful are they?
  How could they be improved? Think about general principles as well as
  practical details.

- *What system of assessment do you think is appropriate for you and your
  work?* Sauce for the goose. On what criteria would you like to be
  judged? This isn't a frivolous exercise. Work out appropriate and fair
  criteria, and then judge yourself. One of the reasons for doing this
  exercise is that there's no point thinking about pupil assessment, the
  effects it might have on them, and the uses to which it can be put,
  without joining in the game ourselves. 'Ourselves' (rather than
  'yourselves') of course includes managers and tutors – so in your self-
  assessments, you may include comments on support, etc., so that your
  self-assessment is contextualised. Formal assessment of teachers
  (appraisal) is now a requirement for most teachers.

Glossary of Key Terms on Assessment

Assessment
Assessing means finding out exactly what a pupil has achieved;
evaluating means making judgements about what the pupil has achieved
and could achieve. In practice, the word 'assessment', alone, is usually
used for both processes. ('Appraisal' usually means assessment of
teachers.)

(National Curriculum) Attainment Targets (ATs)
Broad areas of potential achievement within a subject – e.g. History ATs
originally included understanding cause and effect in History, and dealing
with contrasting historical interpretations (now there is just one AT, called
'History'); English ATs include speaking, listening, reading, writing;
Music ATs include performing/composing and listening/appraising; etc.

Criterion-referenced assessment

Assessing someone according to a list of qualities (criteria) pre-set by the assessor. For example, Level 2 for US Presidents might include the criterion 'can walk and chew gum at the same time'. (Gerald Ford was allegedly assessed by Richard Nixon as being at Level 1.) GCSEs (like the National Curriculum assessments) are supposed to be criterion-referenced – i.e. they are definitely not just supposed to give grades A B and C to the cleverest 40% of the population. (Many people don't quite believe that GCSE really is criterion-referenced. A sensitive point.)

Formative assessment

Assessment done during a course or unit etc., with the aim of helping the pupil to improve – i.e. with the aim of 'forming' future performance.

(National Curriculum) Levels of Achievement

The level reached by the pupil within an attainment target. Level 1 is what an average 5 year old would be at (though the Government insists the levels are not norm-referenced); Level 2 the average 7 year old; 4 the average 11 year old; between 5 and 6 the average 14 year old; between 6 and 7 the average 16 year old. Since Dearing, the 10 level scale has been dropped from Key Stage 4. Nevertheless, the equivalence with GCSE grades, as originally envisaged, may help you to understand the system better. The old nominal equivalence (GCSE grade/NC level) was: A/10 and 9; B/8; C/top 7; D/bottom 7 and top 6; E/bottom 6; F/5; G/4; U/3, 2 and 1.

Marking

The word 'marking' seems curiously old fashioned now, but it still goes on of course. The reason for 'marking' being replaced by 'assessment' in many contexts was a problem with marks themselves. Some schools and departments don't allow teachers to give marks to pupils, either numbers or letters, for the fair reason that work demonstrates far more qualities than can be captured by a single mark. However, pupils themselves may ask for marks, to clarify their progress or their position in the class. Whatever your, or the school's, policy allows, it is worth noting that a mark is only meaningful to a pupil to the extent that the pupil trusts or understands the teacher. A 'C' from a picky or sarcastic teacher may feel like an insult; a 'C' from a supportive and fair teacher may feel like a helpful comment.

Norm-referenced (or normative) assessment

Assessing someone according to how they rank amongst their peers.

Officially considered old-hat, but stubbornly refusing to disappear. Fixing a 'norm', however, leads to assessing some as 'abnormal': this is the most obvious problem with the system.

Profile
A description of the skills, knowledge, understanding, etc., demonstrated by a pupil on a particular course. Profiling is a way of making assessment (especially summative assessment) more meaningful. It has been developed mostly in post-16 education, especially in vocational courses like BTEC, NVQ/GNVQ and the old CPVE. The certificating body will generally give a list of qualities (e.g. 'can pass on a simple message over the phone', or 'can calculate percentages', or 'can participate sensitively in a debate on a controversial issue'), and the profile will consist of the qualities demonstrated and the contexts in which they were demonstrated. For example, 'In the assignment on Nuclear Power, Michelle participated sensitively in the debate on siting a nuclear power station' – or perhaps 'C32b in A24' if all the qualities and contexts are coded. Profiling has crept in to 'academic' courses, and under other names (see below) is central to the National Curriculum/GCSE. There are at least three advantages of profiling. Assessment should be more objective, as other teachers or pupils can easily check up on what skills a pupil has. Assessment is more meaningful – a simple grade is meaningful only if you know the marking scheme, and few pupils/families/employers know marking schemes. Teachers can focus their teaching on the skills, etc. that they feel are important – perhaps those most achievable by the pupils, or those missed out or insufficiently demonstrated earlier in the course. Profiling can look messy, but it can transform teaching methods by making teachers focus on pupils rather than syllabuses. Teachers have to think about what pupils will achieve from a task or course, rather than just what's on the syllabus. Profiling also makes assessment entirely positive – i.e. you list the achievements of the pupil, not their failures or limitations, which are merely implied by what is not said on the profile.

(National Curriculum) Statements of Attainment
A statement representing one particular level of achievement within one Attainment Target. For example, 'put together information drawn from different historical sources', which was the statement of attainment for National Curriculum History Attainment Target 3, level 3.

Summative assessment
Assessment done at the end of a course unit etc., with the aim of summarising the achievements of the pupil on that course. A 'Record of

Achievement' ('ROA' or 'RoA', or NRA for National Record of Achievement, or in London often 'LRA', or, e.g. 'CRA' in Camden) is usually a set of summative assessments, along with certificates (which are simply 'official' and very standardised summative assessments). 'Report' is the old name for a formative and/or summative assessment. You may also write (draft) references. Reports and references tend nowadays to follow the 'positive comments only, plus targets' pattern of criterion-referenced assessment.

Section C

THE TEACHER OUTSIDE THE CLASSROOM

'Man can be educated according to all the exceedingly varied patterns that the contemporary social world offers us today; also he has the capacity not just to submit passively to education, but also to educate himself, and this makes it possible for him to transcend and overstep the training facilities offered him in the direction of the truth' (Alexander Mitscherlich, *Society Without the Father: A Contribution to Social Psychology*, 1963, 1969, p.13)

CHAPTER 12

Developing Schools

National Education Policies

National government policies on education change over the years: both the policies and the rate of change affect schools. This is not the place for a long discussion of current or possible future policies, but all teachers should be aware of the things to look out for in government policies, especially those doing research or with responsibility in school for implementing particular policies. These are four important areas:

- The curriculum in schools is now mostly governed by national policies. Until 1988, only RE was legally obliged to be on the curriculum. Since 1988, the subjects required, and the content of these subjects, have been set out in the National Curriculum.

- Many parts of the 'hidden' curriculum – aspects of the school that affect children but are not parts of 'subjects' – are governed by national policies. On behaviour, certain punishments are banned (including corporal punishment in state schools), others (such as exclusions) should follow strict guidelines. The general well-being of pupils, their moral and spiritual development, is an aim for all teachers.

- Finance has changed the way schools work in recent years. LEA schools are now responsible for a huge proportion of their budgets, which of course affects the power relationships within schools and between schools and LEAs. Money going to schools is now more sensitive to pupil numbers, making the public image of the school, and its ability to attract pupils, even more important: the loss of a dozen pupils may mean the loss of a teacher.

- The status and role of schools can change. After moves towards comprehensive schools in the 1960s and 1970s, many schools are now moving back to selection, or to specialisation (as in the USA). Schools may 'opt out' of LEA control, to become charitable trusts funded by central government at a level related to LEA funding levels. Schools may also 'opt in' from the private sector.

These and many other issues are covered in the education press, and in Department for Education circulars and other publications. They are worth researching: note that it can be difficult getting up-to-date books on very recent policy changes.

Quality and School Improvement

A buzz word is a word that seems, whilst fashionable, to have a power way beyond its meaning. 'Quality' has become such a buzz word in the education system. The word itself (in its current use) comes out of management theory, but the significance of its use in education circles probably lies within the education system itself. There was a time when educationalists (those with power in the system, administrators, heads, academics and politicians with an interest, and so on) fought over ideas such as 'free education for all' or 'comprehensive schools' or 'equality of opportunity', or more recently 'vocationalism'.

However, whilst politicians through the 1980s continued with various grand schemes, many academics and other educationalists influenced by them moved towards apparently smaller-scale and more modest aims. A key book, *Fifteen Thousand Hours* (Rutter *et al.,* 1979), led the way. This book seemed to say that, whatever grand theories and broad trends appeared and disappeared, an individual school might be measurably better or worse than another school at doing things like getting children through exams or encouraging good behaviour. What made the school better or worse in this way was a set of qualities such as the punctuality of teachers, or the system of rewards and sanctions offered by the school. Some academics sniffed, suggesting that these incremental differences between schools were not as important as the direction of the entire system: it was like pointing the way to the first-class cabins in the *Titanic* – an improvement, no doubt, but not a solution to the big problem. However, the approach led by *Fifteen Thousand Hours*, looking at real and achievable ways of judging or improving schools, had a powerful appeal. How can *this* school be improved? Management theories that had been developed over years in industry and private sector services, built on solutions to competitive pressures, were suddenly seen as relevant to schools. Making individual schools take more responsibility for their own finances, and allowing open enrolment so that popular schools could grow, meant that after 1988 work on incrementally improving schools was of huge significance to all schools.

In this climate, 'quality' became a buzz word, and school improvement appears to be the big idea of the 1990s. Institutions in which management systems built around quality set clear aims, generally including profit, and looked at the ways everyone in the institution contributed to meeting those aims. As all schools are dedicated (presumably at least in part) to learning, the quality of learning became a key issue. Mission statements, and mottoes (now in English, not Latin) printed on letter heads, have become fashionable. These general aims should invade all aspects of the work of the institution – including the details of classroom practice and the approach to major policy decisions. If such aims and policies are going to be meaningful, then the importance of engagement in the process, as well as the outcome, can't be emphasised enough. All staff, pupils and others concerned with the school need to be directly involved in the production and promulgation of the overall aims. It is easy to ignore the fact that pupils, teachers, non-teaching staff, parents, and others may have fundamentally different aims, but coming to some sort of agreement can still be a great boon to a school.

Once you commit yourself to quality, you commit yourself to measuring quality – a never-ending process, sometimes called a quality audit. Books like that by MacBeath *et al.* (1992) describe ways of doing qualitative research. There are many ways of doing quantitative research – with a lot of current stress on 'value added' (for example, measuring changes in reading ages), as described by McPherson in the National Commission on Education's Briefings (1993). Quality audits may look at schemes of work, induction and progression processes, systems of assessment (including self-assessment, and including the assessment of staff), and so on. The OFSTED system for inspecting schools, incidentally, follows such procedures. They are likely to look, in particular, at the extent to which general aims and policies are actually implemented in the classroom. Very sensible.

Criticism of 'quality' doesn't just come from those wishing to change the whole course of education (as in the *Titanic* analogy), but also from those who think the term is vacuous. Ted Wragg in the *TES* asked awkward questions like 'What is the opposite of quality?' and 'Has there ever been anyone who wished to promote "unquality" in education?'. To the first type of criticism, it is at least worth pointing out that there were more lifeboats in the first-class sections of the *Titanic*. To the second type of criticism, it is worth admitting that though 'quality' is not anything very new, it is, like 'good', still a word we would like applied to us or our work!

Management and Peer Support

Schools, like many other institutions, tend to be hierarchical. There is a vertical structure of rights and responsibilities. People have rights over those lower in the system (e.g. heads can tell teachers what to do, teachers can tell pupils what to do, etc.), and have responsibilities to those higher in the system (e.g. pupils are reported on by their teachers, teachers are reported on by their managers, etc.). When a school has worked this vertical structure out in complete detail, with every member of staff having one nominated person above them in the hierarchy for each of their responsibilities, the system becomes 'line management'. That is, there are clear 'lines' of responsibility. The ideal form of line management rarely exists – there are usually some 'short cuts': ways of subverting or inverting the system. This doesn't stop schools from claiming they use it.

What line management can ignore is the ways in which people at the same hierarchical level in a school can help each other. This horizontal support (amongst pupils or staff) is always happening, and can be made use of in a more formal way. A third approach, where everyone in a school has a role in supporting the school as a whole, is known as 'collegiality'. This third approach may complement either or both the other two forms of management or support.

What is described here as management and peer support should not be taken as alternative ways of organising a school. A good, formal, line management system can also allow for and encourage good peer support. And peers are not the only people who can support someone in school: management can (and should) be supportive, too.

Principles of Management

The principles of management are important for all teachers, as all teachers are 'managers' of pupils, and need to deal with 'higher up' managers every day. There are many ways of describing management – some described in my bibliography. These are my principles.

● The role of managers should be to support those they manage. Not support in some gushing way – not just 'being nice' – and not support that undermines the professionalism of the people being supported.

Rather, assertive support – related to job descriptions and the overall aims of the institution. I tend to think of hierarchies as inverted triangles. I realised the importance of this when a Principal I used to work with was talking to my tutor group and said something like 'Mr Stern has been working for me for...'. I hadn't until then thought that I had been working for him – I thought that he had been working for me. Good management is that which incorporates the attitude that the institution's managers see themselves as supporting other institution staff, and institution staff see themselves as supporting the institution's students. This is vital. Frank Lloyd Wright had it in one: 'From the ground up makes good sense for building. Beware of from the top down' (quoted in Newton and Tarrant, 1992).

- An important principle should always, of course, be that senior managers be role models for other staff, as staff should be role models for students. This should mean, in practice, that senior managers should set the highest standards in their teaching, and always welcome observation from others, as well as the more obvious models of behaviour and attitude such as being fair, conscientious, hard working and efficient. In such a context, appraisal should be a natural part of the teaching profession, simply an extension of (really just a part of) the duty of managers to support people, helping them set and reach targets, and work as effectively as they can – as teachers try to do with students. I know of no teacher who thinks they can't be helped to improve. Yet the sadness is that appraisal is so often not seen as this, but rather as some prelude to disciplinary procedures or some unwelcome interference. Whether this is a fault of teachers, managers, local authorities, or central government, I'll leave you to work out. But distorting management in this way doesn't half muck it up. Management can work tremendously well even in the most difficult of circumstances. Its effectiveness of course depends on relationships more than formal structures, but formal structures can express relationships too.

Situations for Heads of Department

Each of these situations happen often enough in school. All are likely to provide something for the head of department to do. Work out what you would do, as a head of department, in these circumstances. There may well not be an obvious 'right' answer, or easy solution, of course. The advantage of thinking about these issues at every stage of a career, rather than when or if you become a head of department, is that you will be better able to seek the most appropriate support from others if you have already worked out what you'd do in their shoes. (Some heads of department, when presented with a problem, say 'Well, what would you like me to do?')

- **A teacher says 'Can we have a pupil expelled?'** What would you as head of department need to find out (from the teacher and/or from the pupil)? How would you decide whether or not to go for an exclusion? If you are going to try for one, how would you go about the practical details?

- **A teacher acts in a way that you think is unprofessional.** The teacher says they had a 'rapport' with a pupil, and that it hadn't been a busy day, anyway, so they went off to the shops and bought the pupil some new, trendier, clothes. As head of department, how would you deal with the situation?

- **Two teachers have clearly had a row with each other. They both seem quite upset about the row.** What can you do as head of department? What are your priorities in this situation? As well as what you could do now, in the school, is there anything you could do later?

- **A teacher has had a distressing time in a class. The teacher would like to know what has happened to the class. They ask you to find out.** As head of department, would you want or be able to find this out? How would you go about this and how, too, would you deal with the teacher?

- **Books in your department seem to be going missing at an alarming rate, perhaps because teachers are not keeping track of them.** As head of department, how would you investigate and deal with this situation, without creating a huge overload of work for you or other teachers in the department?

Peer Support

Pupils help each other. Some teachers call this cheating. Sometimes it is cheating, but more often it is what makes a class run smoothly. If you ever teach, or are, a single pupil, you realise what help groups give each other. They support intellectually and emotionally; they give places to hide and sources of alternative entertainment. They also, of course, provide sources of bullying and incentives to avoid success. Nevertheless, the teacher should be able to build on the support offered by pupils to each other, and minimise the damage done.

- Many teachers make the mistake of thinking that a pupil can best get support from friends. The friends of a pupil may support them in many ways, but isn't it strange that everyone can remember a friend who helped them avoid work or be naughty, yet few of us can remember a friend who helped us study harder? Teachers need reminding of that. I'm still surprised, when I get classes to sit in teacher-directed groups, how often individual pupils say to me afterwards 'we worked better like that, don't let us go back to our old seats'. This despite the collective moaning that usually accompanies the suggestion of teacher-directed group work. Classrooms are places of learning, and we can learn more the more people we learn from: that alone is reason enough to get pupils working outside friendship groups. It is also a good reason to have mixed, and mixed-ability, classes. Teachers can use all kinds of techniques to encourage good group work amongst pupils. (Some are described in Chapter 7.) Ideas for varying the groups are just as important as the content of the work itself. Home–expert–home grouping methods have change built in. Other ideas include explaining to pupils the advantages of having mixed groups, and getting them to be responsible for putting themselves in such groups (with the teacher as 'consultant'). Or let pupils divide themselves into pairs (presumably by friendship), with the teacher then putting the pairs together into mixed groups of four. Pupils can in such ways learn effectively from each other in small groups. The whole class can learn from each other, too. Brainstorming sessions and whole-class displays are examples of this. Again, my earlier suggestions about group work and aural or oral work include plenty of ideas.

● More formal kinds of pupil peer support have recently become popular. 'Peer tutoring', where pupils are trained to teach their peers, has been used, for example, to teach about sensitive issues such as HIV/AIDS. The system of having prefects (or form captains, or group representatives) has made use of the same idea for many years. There are many other ways of making effective use of peer support amongst pupils. Think of ones appropriate to your subjects!

● Teachers, like pupils, support each other. It sounds so obvious, yet it is seldom recognised. Heads or Deputies (and managers at every level) sometimes think that they are the source of all support for staff, and that staffrooms are places of subversion and revolt. Well, perhaps, but staffroom 'subversion' – jokes, complaints, and innuendo – is also a means of support, indeed of survival. Find out what support can be found, and make use of it. Try, for example, looking outside your subject/department: try for an inter-departmental trip to a museum, or swap resources on interesting topics. As a History teacher, I can link with English (war poetry), Art (Elizabethan portraiture), Music (nationalist songs), French (legacy of the Revolution), and practically any other subject, if I want to. Every subject specialist tends to think their subject is at the heart of the whole curriculum, but there's no harm in megalomania if it provides a source of interesting peer support.

- More formal peer support amongst teachers includes mutual observation. One of the best INSET sessions I have seen was on teaching techniques, where teachers were asked several weeks in advance to pair up with teachers at the same level in the system, and observe each other's lessons. Because teachers were not being observed by people higher up in the hierarchy, and because they observed and were observed by the same person, they felt comfier with the whole process. And the ideas everyone came up with in the INSET session were much richer for it. Amongst student teachers, mutual observation, again, can be particularly supportive, as it avoids any tinge of assessment. Such peer support can reinvigorate the most jaded of staffs.

- Partnership teaching is also worth considering, where two teachers work with a single class, generally with one having a special responsibility for Special Needs or for Language Development. (This of course needs appropriate funding, unless a student teacher is involved.) It can be a way of thinking about support that avoids the common problem of support teachers having a low status (with both pupils and fellow teachers), and helps professionals to think about their teaching techniques without feeling too threatened. Where I've seen partnership teaching work most effectively, it has involved clear agreements (or contracts) covering the different responsibilities of the different teachers, and ways of monitoring progress.

Display in and Design of Schools

Take all the people out of a school. Now walk around it. Would you like to work there? Would you feel encouraged there? Do you think the children would be happy or stimulated there? Does it look tatty and depressing or exciting and warm? Does it look cared for? Does it look like a place where people care for each other? What does it smell like? Is it dirty, or noisy, or scary?

I'm not sure what a 'good' school is, or what makes it 'good', but I'm sure that I could find out most of what I want to know about a school by looking around it. This section is both a brief guide to practice and a guide to research into practice. Teachers will generally have to adapt their approach to display to the individual characteristics of the school in which they work: depending on the type, amount, and cost of technology, the size of display boards or areas, the school's policies on resources, and so on. If the school has someone responsible for resources (sometimes called a Media Resources Officer, or MRO), they will be a useful person to consult on such issues, as will schoolkeepers, caretakers or site services staff.

Worksheets

If you produce worksheets or handouts for your classes, these need to be effective and should be attractive. Pupils often find worksheets annoying, especially if they get lots of them, perhaps because they feel the teacher is not actually talking to them, perhaps because they are so often unclear and badly reproduced.

- Worksheets should be special. If you can, reproduce them on coloured paper (a pastel shade, not to obscure the writing) or, if they can be re-used, on card. Try to include an illustration as well as text; if there isn't an obvious illustration, perhaps try a fancy border or a departmental or personal letter-heading or motif. A scrappy, old, obscure worksheet is an insult.

- Worksheets should, broadly, follow the rules you would expect of pupils. For example, headings should be underlined, full sentences should be used for instructions, there should be a margin (because of uncertainties of photocopying, it is useful to leave a border around all four edges – faded edges look bad and can make a worksheet meaningless), handwriting and typing should be neat, etc.

- Don't use block capitals for titles, key instructions, (or as some teachers do) the whole worksheet. Block capitals are harder to read than lower-case letters: a word written in block capitals is rectangular in shape, whereas the shape of a word in lower-case letters is uneven, distinctive, and therefore easier to recognise.

- Think about the variety of ways in which people learn. (Think about the way different people do jigsaw puzzles.) Some learn by grasping or trying to grasp the whole picture, and then fit individual bits of information into this picture. Some learn by building up bit by bit, learning distinct things at each stage. (Psychologists may call these 'deep' or 'surface' approaches, or 'conclusion-oriented' or 'descriptive'.) Worksheets often accommodate the style favoured by the teacher, which may be why some have a broad introduction or spidergram and a general task, whereas others have loads of numbered points. Try to mix the styles of your worksheets, to accommodate the styles of learning of your pupils. For example, include a general introduction *and* numbered points, or include a picture or diagram (or spidergram) *as well as* the detailed information.

Classrooms

- The same principles apply to classrooms (including, especially, black- or white-boards) as apply to worksheets: classrooms being special, following rules expected of pupils, forms of lettering, ways of thinking. Apply them.

- Classrooms in primary schools generally look better than classrooms in secondary schools. This is not simply because primary teachers work harder on display, or know more about it. Rather, it is because primary pupils and their teachers tend to stay in the same room for most of the week, and therefore feel that the room is theirs. You are more likely to take care of, and spend time decorating, a room that you feel is yours. In a secondary school, it is worth reproducing this feeling, as much as is possible. You may allocate certain (clearly labelled) areas of wall space as being for the exclusive use of one class or year group; you may make the tutor group who use the room into organisers of the room – perhaps in charge of making sure the displays are in good order, or getting rid of graffiti, or watering plants. You may take photos of your classes (or of key classes) doing their work or on field trips, and mount the photos for heading displays.

- If you can, use plants in the room. Some teachers say that plants are too delicate for their pupils. Most house plants originally grew in tropical forests. Are these teachers saying that the environment in their class is harsher than that in a tropical forest? What does that say about the school's atmosphere? I have found that plants have a calming effect on pupils, who are less likely to run about or throw things because of the risk of damage. Plants certainly make a room look more attractive and homely. Most popular are yukka plants (and the similar dragon plants) and spider plants, with cheese plants and rubber plants close behind. Personally, I'd put in a plea for begonias. Go for plants with attractive foliage, as you are going to want them to look good all year. It would be sensible for the school to have a budget for plants; if they don't, then you could suggest it.

- The classroom should be informative, even without you in it. It should be clear what is being studied in the room (including all the subjects, if there are several), and who is studying it. All rooms must have fire drills in them, and can have school or class behaviour policies, and topic or course descriptions on display. They could also have lists of key words and their definitions, descriptions of assessment criteria, reminders of key skills, etc. History rooms may have timelines, languages rooms may have tourist posters, and so on.

- Pupils should have their work displayed. Even the most disaffected pupil can take pride in their work if it is displayed. The work should be carefully displayed, and looked-after (if corners come unstuck, or lose their drawing pins, repair them immediately), as tattily displayed work is an insult. The work should be from the current topic, so that it is useful and so that people use it. As a rule, change displays 3–6 times a year (i.e. every term or half-term). If you find putting up displays difficult, get pupils to do mini-displays (e.g. putting several bits of work on a large sheet of sugar paper) and then it is easy to put up two or three of these mini-displays.

Schools

- The same principles apply to schools as apply to worksheets and classrooms. Apply them.

- The design of schools varies enormously – a single school may have buildings dating from different centuries, and different schools may have wholly different atmospheres created by the buildings alone. However, the design of the buildings is likely to have less effect than the use made of them. (Rutter *et al.* (1979) found no correlation between the type or state of buildings and any of the school's outcomes.) The general advice is to exploit the school's good points and disguise the school's bad points. For example, tall Victorian rooms may have loads of space for display, to be exploited, but may have poor acoustics, to be disguised (e.g. by using carpets – including old throw-away rugs, curtains, or soft displays).

- Pupils should feel safe throughout the school. A good exercise is to get pupils to mark on a map of the school where bullying is most likely to take place. (Most often, in toilets and unsupervised outdoor areas.) Teachers should be aware of the whole school: it isn't much good making all the classrooms friendly and educational if pupils are terrified to walk down the corridors or go to the toilet. Sometimes there are design solutions to problems around the school; more often, it is a matter of supervision and systems of dealing with bullying.

- The school should reflect both the people who use it (pupils and staff) and the environment surrounding the school. Whole school displays should tell people about pupils and about the area. The community studies I suggest in the research section (see Chapter 4) would make good displays, for example. Local groups may wish to use the school to do displays of their own, and the school may wish to do displays for local libraries or shop windows. The Hargreaves Report (ILEA, 1984) talks sensibly about how unwelcoming many schools are, and the bad effects this can have on parents and other visitors.

CHAPTER 13

Developing People in Schools

The Progression of Pupils: Transfer at 5, 11 and 16

All education involves change and therefore progression. Schools tend to mark changes in particular ways – for example, with bells between lessons or assemblies to start the day. Some changes have special significance.

- Going to school for the first time, usually at 4 or 5. The change is from education being provided relatively informally by family, friends and the mass media, to education being provided by authoritative strangers, amongst strange peers, in formal situations. The shock of this change may turn intelligent, curious and talkative children into inarticulate and apparently stupid pupils (as Salmon, 1988, Chapter 3, describes). Some never get over the change, as John Holt (Holt, 1969) describes of older primary pupils. Teachers should never forget the strangeness of what they are doing.

- Changing school at 11 is the next huge change. (Some authorities and schools transfer at other ages, but 11 is by far the most popular primary–secondary split.) Primary schools usually keep pupils with one teacher most of the time, and pupils are likely to have a more integrated programme of learning (often not repeated until pupils enter post-16 courses). Secondary schools, which may be several times larger than primary schools, tend to divide the day up into short periods, with pupils changing teachers four or five or more times a day. A relatively integrated programme of learning may be split into anything up to a dozen quite distinct subjects, each following its own rules and programmes of study. Teaching is likely to be more formalised (or 'strict', as primary pupils tend to describe it, fearfully) and, sadly, less investigative, experiential, and pupil-centred. Secondary teachers tend to think this form of organisation is inevitable, and seldom see or practise the techniques used by primary teachers, and used again by many teachers in further education. A useful research activity for secondary teachers, then, is to visit and observe these different schools, and to ask young secondary, or old primary, pupils about their hopes and fears about the transfer at 11. Always informative, the results of such research can be used to make secondary schools more effective and supportive.

- At 16, the change is more complicated. Those pupils who carry on into the sixth form of their secondary school may notice little change, except an increase in privileges and a decrease in the number of subjects studied. Those pupils who go on to sixth form, tertiary, or FE colleges, or who go on to training schemes or jobs including training, will have more to cope with. The biggest change is the legal one: schooling is still a right for 16–19 year-olds, but it is not compulsory. This can have a big psychological effect on both pupils and teachers. People who volunteer to learn can be expected to behave differently, in all sorts of ways.

The second biggest change is likely to be in the curriculum. For 11–16 year-olds, the curriculum is likely to be made up of many discrete academic subjects. After 16, the curriculum is likely to be more specialised, and may be tied to particular jobs or groups of jobs, i.e. it may become 'vocational' rather than 'academic'. There are moves to bring more vocational education into Key Stage 4 (for 14–16 year-olds) in schools, and this may reduce the shock of the changes at 16. In many ways, as I've said earlier, courses for pupils after 16, especially vocational courses, may resemble the primary curriculum: they may be integrated (i.e. someone may try to make all the different elements fit together), they may be investigative and pupil-centred, with teachers acting more as tutors than lecturers. Attempts to unify post-16 education, with a single qualification covering academic and vocational courses, may make academic courses (currently A levels) more like vocational courses.

Again, as secondary teachers tend to think their form of organisation is inevitable, and seldom see or practise the techniques used by FE teachers, a useful research activity would be to visit and observe FE colleges, and to ask 15–17 year olds about their hopes and fears concerning experiences of the transfer at 16.

To avoid the loss of skills and knowledge at these or other periods of transfer, it is worth thinking about how to acknowledge prior learning and experience. In further education, schemes of APL (the accreditation of prior learning) have been introduced. The principles of APL can be used by all teachers, though: starting any course by brainstorming pupils on their prior knowledge is a simple and effective method. It is worth noting the dangers of loss in transfer at even the smallest level. In secondary schools, a change of lesson, perhaps after less than an hour, may need to be followed by reasserting rules or procedures, and re-capping old knowledge. Salzberger-Wittenberg *et al.* (1983) looked at the psychology of change, and how to cope with it. Every ending (even the end of a lesson) is like a small bereavement.

Pupils and Teachers Becoming Adult: Transactional Analysis (TA)

The theories of TA were developed by the American army psychiatrist Eric Berne, initially in his book *'Games People Play: The Psychology of Human Relationships'*, written in 1964 (Berne, 1968). Its foundations are broadly Freudian, but, unlike Freud's massive and complex theories, TA can be used effectively and appropriately, by anyone who works with people, to analyse and develop strategies for dealing with quite simple situations. There are three basic ways of acting in a situation, he says: as a 'parent' (roughly the Freudian superego), as an 'adult' (the Freudian ego) or as a 'child' (the Freudian id). Complementary transactions are either adult–adult (e.g. surgeon puts out hand for scalpel, nurse puts handle of scalpel in surgeon's hand) or parent–child (e.g. ill child asks for a glass of water, nurturing parent brings it). Similar complementary transactions are parent–parent (e.g. what Berne calls 'critical gossip': 'Young people today are all delinquents' – 'Yes, and they aren't taught any manners at home either') and child–child (e.g. children playing cops and robbers). Complementary transactions can go on indefinitely. However, communication breaks down when a crossed transaction occurs. For example, the 'adult–adult' question 'Where are my cuff links?' might be responded to with the 'child–parent' 'You always blame me for everything!' (instead of the 'On the desk' 'adult' reply). Then, either the first person changes their role into that of the complementary 'parent' (in this example), or the second person comes around to the complementary 'adult' role. This realignment could take seconds or it could take years, or it could never happen.

Let's look at school situations:

P: Gulden, your homework was rubbish.	P
A	A
C	C: Yes miss. I'm sorry miss. I'll try to do better in future.

That was complementary. This next one isn't, because Gulden makes a child–child response:

P: Gulden, your homework was rubbish.	P
A	A
C	C: I don't care, I thought the work was boring anyhow.

Try continuing that conversation. This next example isn't complementary, either, because Gulden makes an adult–adult response:

P: Gulden, your homework was rubbish.	P
A	A: What is it exactly that you feel is poor?
C	C:

Try continuing that one. The next one has the teacher starting an adult–adult transaction, but with the pupil giving a child–parent response:

How do you think you would continue, as a teacher? What about an

P:	P
A: Now, where do you think the problem lies?	A:
C	C: Miss, will you do this for me?

adult–adult opening, with a child–child response – the next example. I'll leave you to work out the further significance of all this!

P:	P
A: What would it take for you not to feel so bored? What is it I do which makes you feel this way?	A:
C	C: This lesson's boring. You make me sick.

Work out your own favourite answers to some of the typical statements by pupils, and listen out, in everyday life as well as in teaching, for the different types of response. Moving towards adult–adult interactions with pupils – and with teachers – means moving towards maturity. This is always important to remember in schools, where too many people get stuck in childishness or immaturity.

Self Awareness and Self-Esteem: Emotional and Psychological Blocks to Learning

● *Study yourself* – Think about how you react, for example, to failure, to loss, to anger, to criticism, to being ignored or unsupported, to being condescended to, or to loneliness. What events or situations make you feel encouraged, bothered, afraid? Think about how you react to the opposite set of situations. Think about what helps you, in the difficult situations, and what negates the effects of the positive situations. (A very simple test: what does it feel like to be shouted at, at close range?)

Now, think about what you want to do in the classroom, and think about what you actually do there. (A simple follow-up test: do you ever shout at pupils at close range?) Think about how you react to particular classes or pupils – what do you feel like? As a rule of thumb, the best way to understand what a class (or an individual pupil) thinks about you, is to work out how *you* feel about *them*. For some reason, people seem to make you feel how they feel. If you feel angry (or frustrated, or encouraged, or stupid, or depressed) with a pupil or class, it is likely that they already feel angry (or frustrated, etc.) with you, and that is why they have made you feel the way you do. Teachers may be in control of the curriculum, but, often, pupils are in charge of the emotional state of the teachers. Think about it. It can be useful being honest, and confronting issues. For example, you might say 'Look, I can see by the way you're behaving that you must find some of this work frustrating, but it is something we both have to do, for a couple of weeks, so that we can get quickly onto the next (presumably exciting) piece of work'.

What is self-esteem? How do you work out who has more or less self-esteem? Think about the self-esteem of your pupils and, please, think about your own self-esteem. The level of self-esteem of a teacher is the best guide to how well they are likely to support the pupils. It is also the best guide to how adaptable or resilient a teacher is likely to be – i.e. how well they can recover from, and learn from, their mistakes. Teachers with low self-esteem are more likely to get stuck in a bad pattern of working.

- *Study the books* – Look up each of these books in my bibliography. I've included brief descriptions of them, though it would of course be better if you picked out one or two and looked at the books themselves. The book I find most useful (one of my favourites, anyway) is Salzberger-Wittenberg *et al.* (1983). These books (in alphabetical order) also deal with many of the issues, in different ways: Bargh, 1987; Berne, 1968; Besag, 1989; Burns, 1982; D'Albert, 1989; Fontana, 1986; Goffman, 1968; Griffin, 1985; Gross, 1987; Gross, 1990; Hargreaves, 1972; Lennox, 1991.

- *Study yourself again* – Keep thinking about the emotional and psychological aspects of teaching and learning. If you do, you've got the best chance of becoming (never 'being') a better teacher. It is particularly important to think about, and try to sort out, these aspects of teaching or learning at the times when you are feeling bad about the job, or just feeling bad. (And remember, it is only a job.)

Pupils and Teachers Staying in Control: Time Planning and Stress Management

There is a joke, along the lines that 'I don't have the time or energy to work on time management or stress management'. (See also: 'I've been too ill to see the doctor'.) If you say you have no time to do time planning, it means you actually enjoy being totally stressed out. If you don't enjoy the stress, then plan your time. Bear in mind that I am one of the world's worst worriers. I could worry for Britain in the Olympics. I still, though, find my own advice useful – otherwise I'd be depressed, suicidal, or both.

Basics

There are 168 hours in a week. The average teacher, according to recent research, works 52 hours a week – which leaves 116 hours to sleep, eat, wash, travel, and have fun in, which isn't too bad. Yes, I know 52 hours a week is far more than the current British average week's work, but (don't tell my boss this) it isn't unusual or, historically, excessive. (Incidentally, the average time spent by a mother of a young child, in Britain, with no paid work, doing housework and childcare, is 77 hours a week. Think on.)

Three reasons why teaching seems to take up 168 hours a week

- Although you may 'only' do 52 hours a week, many people (including, especially, the pupils, the school's managers, and the Department for Education) think you can or should do far more. You never get the impression that you have completed your work, even if you work 167 hours a week. This is, of course, ridiculous – yet many teachers are genuinely convinced that they are not doing enough, however much they do. You are doing enough. Enough is enough; 52 hours a week is already far too much. Sod it. At midnight, you'll turn into a pumpkin anyway – or at least you'll look like one the next morning if you carry on working.

- There will be weeks – especially in your first year of teaching, and in future years near report-writing deadlines, inspection visits, etc. – when you will indeed be working close to 168 hours. Even if this is the result of bad planning, the memory sticks.

- Teaching always involves responsibility, and tends to require commitment. Responsibility and commitment bring with them worry. (They also make the job worthwhile.) Many teachers spend 52 hours a week working and 116 hours a week worrying, including, when asleep, having nightmares. This then feels like 168 hours work. Worry is about the past or the future. Why worry about the past, when you can't change it? Why worry about the future, when you can do something about it? If you can do something about the future, then do it; if you really can't do something about the future, then, as with the past, why worry? In general, an hour's work early in the evening saves 3 hours' worrying later in the evening; 3 hours' worrying followed by an hour's work is equivalent to (i.e. feels like) 4 hours' work. One hour's work followed by 3 hours' fun feels like a lot of fun. Ultimately, I'm told, all small fears or worries are really just premonitions of the fear of death. Maybe you should think about your attitude to your own death, the meaning of life, etc. Mind you, that's hardly a cure for insomnia, is it?

What won't make the job more bearable?

Being nasty to the children you teach. Being nasty to the teachers you work with. Drink. Drugs (including tranquillisers, beta-blockers, pain-killers, sedative cold/'flu cures, etc.). Worry. Promotion. Money (money can be very useful at getting rid of other stresses like bills, but it still doesn't affect the job of teaching itself).

What will make the job more bearable?

Being nasty *about* the children you teach, as long as they can't hear you. (Referring to a pupil who has difficulty with their work as 'jellybrain' may be an appalling insult, but such evil humour, *amongst friends,* may just save you from cracking up.) Being nasty *about* the teachers you work with (though watch out for the staff-room spy – yes, every school seems to have at least one – who will relay any insults of the managers straight to them). Having a diary, and lots of lists.

My theory: 'Lazy' means you enjoy doing nothing, and this is a good quality; 'idle' means you do nothing, and this is a bad quality. Teaching will be more bearable if you don't get the two mixed up. Arnold Bennett obviously had it sussed, using the word 'indolence' for what I mean by 'laziness'. In *Hilda Lessways*, he says of Mr Orgreave 'He was one of the most industrious men in the Five Towns, and assuredly the most industrious architect; but into an idle hour he could pack more indolence than even Johnnie and Jimmie, alleged wastrels, could accomplish in a week'.

Just remember: 'Unhappy, stressed workaholics are not good role models for young people and are unlikely to retain the good humour and positive attitudes required' (Newton and Tarrant, 1992).

It is worth working with pupils on time and stress management, after you have worked on it yourself. This may be especially welcome for pupils with a high proportion of non-contact time – for example, those on 'study leave' before GCSEs, or those studying for A levels – but should be useful for all pupils.

Becoming a Teacher

Finding and Applying for a Job

The *TES* (*Times Educational Supplement*, dated Friday of each week – expect to have gone through it by the end of the weekend) is the place where virtually all jobs are advertised. Other sources will generally be duplicated in the *TES*. Once you have found and preferably bought (so you can cut it up) your *TES*, follow this plan:

1 Have a separate file for your job applications.

2 Start this file with three documents:
  (a) a curriculum vitae including addresses, qualifications, referees, etc.;
  (b) a covering letter ('I would like to apply…Please could you send me…I enclose a CV…');
  (c) a 200-300 word statement about what you've done which is relevant to a job (including how you've applied your principles) and what you would like to do in a job.
  All of these, of course, will need to be, indeed must be, adapted to suit each job you apply for.

3 Keep a record of all the applications you make, including the original advert (dated), any letters or CVs you have sent, and information you put on the application form. It is a nightmare to be invited for an interview without remembering what the job is, exactly, or what you told them about yourself. Some schools will, and all schools can, treat adverts, 'further details' sent to you, and application forms as part of your contract. You are unlikely to get any more detailed contract, at least until your Appraisal comes up. Keep all this after you've started the job, too.

4 Look at the *TES* classified section. Note and understand the categories, which currently include the following:
  (a) Secondary, subject classification (and perhaps SEN), SNS.
  (b) Grant Maintained.
  (c) Sixth Form Colleges.
  (d) Special Schools (different from SEN jobs in mainstream schools).
  (e) Scottish jobs.

(f) Independent schools.

(g) FE and Tertiary.

(h) 'The bit at the end', including overseas, etc.

(i) Block adverts, by school or by LEA, which may be placed anywhere in the classified section.

5 Edit down the job adverts by place (if you can't move from your area), religion, sex, status, etc. Work out your principles (or lack of them) before you apply. Never apply for a job you don't want, and only apply for a job you can convince yourself you can do well – this will save time, energy, and 'the worst mistake I ever made in my life' type situations. Your union should be able to tell you about your pay, although LEAs and schools are notorious for interpreting national guidelines in different ways, especially when it comes to recognising qualifications and experience. As a rough guide, SNS (Standard National Scale, which used to be called Main Professional Grade) in September 1994, for a year's work, was £12,999 for basic, good honours, graduates, with increments to £31,323 (though most teachers would be barred well before this); London allowances were £1,899 to £486 (depending on how central); extra allowances of about £750 to £1200 are given by many inner London LEAs. So an inner London start was about £15,700 a year; a non-London start was about £12,999. Look out, as well, for sweeteners – money to cover removal expenses (which can be worth thousands of pounds), extra allowances, etc. What used to be called Incentive Allowances (for example, for being a head of department) are now simply put into the scale of increments. Hence you might get two extra increments for a post of responsibility than you would otherwise get. This level of pay, and these allowances, cover just about all jobs, except Heads and Deputy Heads, in LEA controlled schools, although there are some other possible discretionary payments. Once you get into Grant Maintained (opted out) schools, or the independent sector, it all gets very complicated. Be prepared to ask, and negotiate.

6 Expect to ring for further information, at the same time as writing with a CV and covering letter. Belt and braces. The further information may include a school prospectus, a job description, and, if you're lucky, a list of selection criteria. If selection criteria are included, then the school is generally obliged to use these criteria alone in making the appointment. You must, therefore, explain in your application how you meet each of the criteria – i.e. what you have done, not just what you believe. Never assume that people will know, or guess, what you believe or have done!

7 Try to arrange a visit to the school. This will make it possible to adapt

your application form to the special conditions in the school.

8 Fill in the application form. Fill it in exactly as they ask, and neatly, even if all the information is also on your CV, and always make the application relevant to the particular job applied for. Because it is easy to get the form wrong (e.g. writing your GCSEs where your A levels should be, or not leaving enough room to put your degree in), it is worth photocopying the form before you write anything, and practising on the photocopy before you do the real thing. This also, incidentally, leaves you with a convenient copy for reference. If the form doesn't allow for some useful information about yourself, you can always write in 'further details on my CV, enclosed'.

9 Post the application (in time for the closing date), then forget about it until you get an interview, at which time get out all your paperwork!

Being Interviewed for a Job

The British education system, like so many others, is based on a culture of failure: however successful you are, you will be made constantly aware of, fearful of, and guilty about, your (possible or actual) failures: 'To be successful in our culture one must learn to dream of failure' (Jules Henry, quoted by Hargreaves, 1982). This is an appalling state of affairs. For pupils, at least, we are at last moving towards promoting their positive qualities – for example in profiles – rather than stressing their limitations or failures. Maybe, with formal teacher appraisal coming into schools, we will move towards a more positive approach to assessing teachers. Interviews, however, haven't really got that far. It may be a good idea to take with you to an interview examples of good work you have done – plans, handouts, analyses, reports, or whatever – but you may well not be asked to show them. Some interviews are preceded by a 'presentation', where you give a pre-prepared answer to a question set by the school; some schools ask candidates to teach a lesson. Presentations and sample lessons may be scary, but they are at least closer to the reality of teaching than is a standard interview. Whatever system is used, bear in mind these rules:

● *Rule One – They want you more than you want them.* Well, they (are likely to) want you more than you (are likely to) want them. Good teachers are in short supply. You are a good teacher, well trained, committed, interested, with valuable experience both in teaching and beyond. If they don't appoint you, it will either be because they're stupid (in which case you didn't want a job there anyway), or because you didn't want the job there anyway.

- *Rule Two – Rehearsed speeches sound false.* Never rehearse specific answers to individual questions, unless you are doing a presentation (and even presentations should sound a little spontaneous). Laurence Olivier himself wouldn't sound convincing with a scripted answer to an interview question; especially if the interviewer innocently believes they have just thought up a totally original question, never before heard. (Remember that a smooth, unfaltering, rehearsed-sounding, answer is in general a sign of a person lying.)

- *Rule Three – Have principles.* Just as you shouldn't *rehearse* answers, you *should* think about your basic principles. What do you believe good teaching is all about? Why do you think mixed-ability (or set/streamed) teaching is valuable? What is so important about equal opportunities, or literacy across the curriculum, or SEN, or the National Curriculum, or whatever? If you've got your basic principles sorted out, you should be prepared to answer any interview question thrown at you. At least, if you follow rule four.

- *Rule Four – Refer to good practice.* Never just talk about theory. Always say how you have (or could have) applied your principles. ('Equal opportunities in practice is an important way of raising self-esteem. For example, if a child is made fearful of answering questions because others in the class, then…'.) Half theory, half practice is a good guide to the balance of what you say in interviews. Learn about the school, too, so that your answers apply to its specific conditions. You may need to do some spying. Mind you, avoid excessive circumlocution – they aren't appointing a professor of educational studies. Keep your answers reasonably short and lively (without the jokes). All interviewers get terribly bored.

- *Rule Five – Prepare for their (rehearsed) speeches and questions.* They are likely to ask you, during the interview, whether you would accept the job if offered to you: say yes. They are also likely to ask if you have any questions you would like to ask them: have one ready (preferably a reasonably interesting but non-controversial one), or at least say 'I had quite a few questions, but you've been so helpful today that…' If you don't get offered the job, you will probably get the set speech: 'It was an exceptionally good field of interviewees today, we would have been happy to appoint any one of you – and we don't normally say that. It was a pleasure meeting you all. You really were unlucky, and I'm sure, with your qualifications and experience, that you'll have no trouble getting a job.' It is worth asking politely for a more detailed breakdown, or 'debriefing'. This may be painful, but should help with the next interview.

Interview Questions

Here are a few common questions I've heard or asked. You are unlikely to be asked more than 10 or 12 of them in one interview.

Did you have a good journey?
How did you find the school? (Both meanings of 'find'.) [†]
You've seen the school. Was it different to your expectations? [†]
How do our pupils compare with those at your (or your TP) school? [†]
What makes a good teacher (or head of department, or whatever)?
What do you think about becoming a teacher?
What about teaching most bothers/interests/frustrates/angers you?
As a teacher, what would you say are your best qualities?
As a teacher, what would you say are your worst qualities?
How do you think you work as a member of a team?
What effect does the way a teacher/pupil dresses have on schooling?
Tell us about a book that you've found useful for your teaching.
What research have you done that would be useful in the classroom?
What do you think of the London A level syllabus we use here?
What would your priorities be for developing Key Stage 3? [†]
How could you contribute to the promotion of this school? [†]
If we turned you down, why do you think it would be? [†]
What can you offer us that is different from the other candidates? [†]
Tell us about a lesson that you were proud of – that went well.
What do you think of SATs?
Select one topic, and say how you would approach teaching it.
Why do you think it is important to teach children about
Science/PE/History/etc.?
How would you cope with a parent who thought your subject was useless?
Given unlimited money, what would your spending priorities be? [†]
If I were to walk past your classroom window, what would I see?
How would you cope with our more quiet/challenging/etc. pupils? [†]
What qualities do you think a tutor needs?
There's plenty of prejudice about. How do you deal with it?
The department has lots of policies/rules. How do you deal with them? [†]
I see you did O level Physics. Might you (want to) teach it here? [*]
How could you contribute to our PSE programme? [*†]

How could you involve parents more in the education of their children?

How could you make use of the community more in your teaching? †

Do you have any questions you'd like to ask us? †

If we were to offer you the job, would you accept it?

* Semi-trick questions, with contractual implications.

† Question for which you'll need to have researched the school.

Record any other interview questions you have been asked, or have heard about other people being asked, for help in future interviews.

Selection Criteria

The selection criteria may have been included in the information sent to you – in which case, make sure you demonstrate how you fulfil them. If not, then the school may still have a set of selection criteria, probably based on the job description, job advert, school development plan, or pressures from outside the school (e.g. from the LEA). For some jobs the interviewing panel will simply have a tick-list, with the candidates' names across the top and the selection criteria down the side. Clearly, some schools will have 'hidden' criteria – such as a preference for appointing a woman, or someone who is a tough disciplinarian – which they may not want to make explicit. You can't predict such criteria, and it isn't really worth trying. Between the ages of 29 and 33, I was told, alternately and with no reason, that I was either too old or too young for the jobs I applied for. (Incidentally, the average age at appointment of London Headteachers is – or at least was – in the early 30s. Frightening, isn't it?) It beats me why age should matter. Knowledge, skill, qualifications, experience, and so on, are obvious – but age? As I've already said, you should find it useful to ask for a debriefing, preferably with the Head. Ask for one. This is the only way you will find out why you didn't (or indeed did) get the job.

If you suspect that you have been discriminated against, remember that there are only two types that are illegal – sexual discrimination and racial/ethnic discrimination. Discrimination might be direct (e.g. 'we're not appointing you because you're a woman') or indirect (e.g. 'we're not appointing you because you'll probably take lots of time off to look after your children when they're ill'). If you suspect this is happening, or has happened, seek immediate advice from your union (if you've got one) and/or the EOC/CRE. If you feel you may in the future be subject to discrimination, seek advice in advance. These are examples of commonly (legitimately) used selection criteria:

- Relevant qualifications for the particular job.

- Knowledge of subject, including National Curriculum, exam syllabuses, etc.

- Knowledge of wide range of relevant teaching techniques, materials, etc.

- Administrative abilities, experience, etc.

- Experience of work with or knowledge of this particular type of school.

- Work with or knowledge of the type of pupils at the school.

- Commitment to LEA or school Equal Opportunities policies.

- Understanding the role of the tutor.

- Possible contribution to school beyond the subject.

- Ability to work with colleagues (in practice, does the Head of Department like you?).

- Flexibility, initiative, enthusiasm, etc. (i.e. manner at interview).

Please record any other selection criteria you have been told about, or have heard about.

Being a Teacher: Legal and Professional Matters

Several legal and professional issues are mentioned in other sections of this book, for example on medical matters, religion, and research. Here, I would like to include some more information on these issues. I couldn't hope to provide comprehensive advice, and it is therefore appropriate to start by recommending that any teacher should join a professional association or union, all of which provide a range of legal and professional support and advice, along with insurance cover in case things go wrong. As with other forms of insurance, it is too late to join once you get into difficulties!

Professionalism

Ask a teacher whether they are professional, or whether they belong to a profession, they will say they are or do; ask a teacher what it means to be professional, they will have difficulty answering. Academic definitions tend to stress specialised academic training and qualifications, high ethical standards enforced by the profession itself, an attitude of 'disinterestedness' and of service to the public, relative autonomy over work, and so on. Teaching, by such definitions, is only partially a profession, as it has little direct control over entrance to the profession, and has no disciplinary powers over itself. However, there are attempts to make teaching more of a profession, and there certainly are 'professional standards' expected of teachers, which have implications for disciplinary matters. A simple, relatively non-controversial, example would be the expectation that teachers do not have sex with their pupils. Codes of professional conduct are not always well publicised. Here is the NUT's code of professional conduct (1993), given as an example:

'The following is a list of actions already declared to be unprofessional but this list is not exclusive. All actions which are alleged to be injurious to the interests of the profession or the professional honour of any member can be referred to the Committee for adjudication.

(a) For any teacher to take an appointment from which in the judgement of the NUT Executive, a member of the Union has been unjustly dismissed.

(b) For any teacher to make a report on the work or conduct of another teacher without at the time acquainting the teacher concerned with the nature of it, if it be a verbal report, or without showing it, if it be written and allowing the teacher concerned to take a copy of it.

(c) In any case of dispute between members of the NUT settled by arbitration under Rule 52 for any member not to abide by the decision.

(d) For any teacher to censure other teachers or to criticise their work in the hearing of the pupils and other persons not directly involved in the running of the school.

(e) For any teacher to seek to compel another teacher to perform outside the ordinary school hours any task which is not essentially connected with the ordinary work and organisation of the school.

(f) For any teacher to impose upon another teacher, out of the ordinary school hours, an excessive or unreasonable amount of work of any kind.

(g) For any teacher to behave in a racially, discriminatory manner or to make racist remarks directed towards or about ethnic minority groups or members thereof.

(h) For any teacher to harass sexually another teacher or pupil.

(i) For any teacher to behave in a discriminatory manner towards, or engage in harassment of others because of their sexual identity.'

Contracts

All teaching jobs involve contracts; most teachers don't see their contracts. Those employed as teachers in LEA controlled schools will almost certainly be covered by the School Teachers' Pay and Conditions Document, 1988. This outlines professional duties and working time. Professional duties include preparing lessons, teaching, assessing, providing guidance, keeping records, communicating with parents and outside organisations, taking part in appraisal, maintaining good order and discipline, attending meetings, doing cover lessons in some circumstances, preparing pupils for exams, taking part in management, doing miscellaneous administration, registering pupils, and so on. Working time describes the 190 days on which a teacher may (note 'may') be required to teach, and a further 5 days on which a teacher may be required to attend for other purposes. It also says that a teacher can be directed to work for 1265 hours, though they may be required to 'work such additional hours as may be needed to enable him to discharge effectively his professional duties, including, in particular the marking of pupils' work, the writing of reports on pupils and the preparation of lessons, teaching material and teaching programmes'. 1265 hours on its own would be an easy contract, implying a 32½ hour week for 39 weeks of the year. No such luck. The 'additional hours' on average mean that teachers work around 52 hours a week (i.e. around 2000 hours a year, not 1265). (This means that if an average teacher spread their work out over the holidays, working a 40-hour week – which is still higher than the British average working week – they would have only two weeks of holidays. If they worked 35 hours a week, they would have to work 57 weeks a year. So much for teachers having short hours and long holidays!)

Contracts will have, or will imply, a specific job description too, although this job description can be changed by the school. Job descriptions are interesting, and are worth asking for, particularly as issues relating to job descriptions can come up at difficult times. Is putting on the school play a part of the job description of the head of drama? Do you help out with the library as a favour or as part of your job description? As a head of subject within a larger faculty, are you the responsible person who will be accounting for that subject to inspectors? Are you responsible for the display cabinets in your corridor, or have you just happened to put up a lot of displays recently?

Many teachers are on temporary or part-time contracts, which have further legal implications. Some legal employment rights do not come into effect until you have been employed for 2 years: don't assume that teaching is a completely 'safe' profession!

Health and Safety

Health and safety issues – too often seen as quite separate from other educational issues – should be acknowledged by all teachers. Too often it is only teachers of subjects with obvious health and safety implications (like technology or PE) who even consider the issues. Yet no teacher wishes to endanger themselves or their students, and they most certainly don't wish to be disciplined, sued or prosecuted as a result of bad health and safety practice. Similarly, all teachers would like support to deal with stress and other common occupational hazards of teaching. Health and safety regulations are and should be seen as more than an imposed set of annoying regulations. 1974 legislation (the Health and Safety at Work Act, 1974) introduced the concept of the general duty of care, rather than just being a list of regulations related to specific equipment and practices. Employers have a duty to set up procedures *and* to enforce them – including if necessary dismissing staff who do not comply. Staff who break the rules may also be guilty of the criminal offence of having 'failed to co-operate'. Job descriptions are again important: if you are responsible for looking after the stock cupboard, and someone is injured by a pile of books falling on them, are you responsible? Can you be sued? Health and safety issues are very wide-ranging, covering car parks, fires, personal belongings, insurance, entertainment licences, liquor (did you bring in wine for your end of term party with pupils under 18?), waste, storage, asbestos, noise, lighting, food, first aid (who in the school is the first aider?), smoking, alcoholism, AIDS, and even stress. Incidentally, don't ask pupils to do potentially dangerous things, like standing on a table to put up a display, or climbing on a roof to retrieve a ball, unless you are happy to risk the professional and/or legal consequences.

Relationships

Professionalism has implications for relationships, many of which are described above in the NUT code of conduct. Here are some points for starters:

● Relationships with other teachers should be professional, in the sense that personal feelings (including liking or disliking someone) should not affect the working relationship. It is unreasonable, for example, to fail to do work asked of you by someone you dislike but who has a right to ask you to do the work. Be wary of criticism (as the NUT points out), and try to avoid getting into feuds, even when these do not affect your work. Harassment or bullying, by or of you, is unprofessional and should be dealt with very quickly. (Sadly, sometimes easier said than done: if you are worried and don't know what to do, at least keep a clear, dated, record of all the incidents that concern you.)

- Relationships with non-teaching staff are often handled badly by teachers. Only about half the staff of a school will be teaching staff, yet teachers who treat teaching colleagues and pupils supportively and with respect can often be off-hand or unreasonable when it comes to non-teaching staff. Cleaners, schoolkeepers/caretakers, office staff, technicians, classroom support workers, ground staff, coach drivers, caterers, and the other non-teaching staff, help the school to run just as much as teachers do. They do not work for teachers; they, like you, work for the school and therefore for the pupils. Non-teaching staff are also likely to know as much about how the school is and could be run as any teacher: they can offer invaluable advice, if asked, and are likely to have made clear, usually accurate, judgements about the various skills and work of the teaching staff. Of course, treating non-teaching staff like colleagues has implications for non-teaching staff, too. They should be involved in (creating and implementing) school policies, for example on racism or sexism, and should have opportunities to take part in INSET and other pupil-centred training.

- Relationships with pupils should be professional, in the sense that, however they behave, you should treat pupils with respect and care, and should support their education as best you can. Remember that pupils between 5 and 16 have no option but to come to school: it is you, not the pupils, who have voluntarily committed yourself to behave professionally. Difficulties can arise if you are unpleasant to pupils, but they can also arise if you appear to build up too close a relationship with an individual pupil. Teachers, especially male teachers, should not be alone with a pupil. If this is unavoidable, then the teacher should inform a colleague. This is to avoid unwarranted accusations of sexual or physical misconduct, and it is also to avoid *warranted* accusations of sexual or physical misconduct. Who is most likely to abuse a child sexually? First on the list are members of the child's family, followed by family friends, followed by teachers.

- There are many other people and organisations that teachers come into contact with, including parents, the school's Governing Body, social workers, police, educational psychologists, visiting speakers, local newspapers, employers taking pupils on work experience, museums or galleries where pupils are taken on trips, and so on. It would be difficult to give advice on every eventuality, but I would say three things:

  – you are employed to work in and for a school, and the school (and its pupils) should therefore have the highest priority, and you (like the pupils) 'represent' the school to outsiders;

– confidentiality is the safest bet when outside organisations seek information;

– people outside the school may well have expertise and knowledge which should never be dismissed.

Once you are out of school, you too may wish to influence schools: as a parent, or a governor, or a local resident, or whatever, you are likely to understand better the relationship between teachers and outsiders. Think about this. Incidentally, once you are out of school, you may think that professionalism no longer matters. It does, although it is rather more limited. It would be unreasonable to ignore serious crime or misbehaviour by pupils when you and they are outside school, although, of course, you should not be expected to deal with it there and then. A quiet word when back in school, with pupil and tutor, should be enough: allow someone else to make the decision about how to proceed.

Section D
DIFFERENT PERSPECTIVES ON EDUCATION

'I had looked into a great many books, which were not commonly known at the Universities, where they seldom read any books but what are put into their hands by their tutors' (Samuel Johnson, quoted in Boswell's *Life*)

CHAPTER 14

Different Views on Different Topics

This chapter includes lists of and some very brief comments on books that I've found particularly useful or interesting. Further details on all these books, and many more books, are included in Chapter 15.

My Top Ten Education Documents

This is certainly not a cross-section of books or films covering the whole of education. It is very definitely a personal choice, based on my own feelings of pleasure at finding documents that are useful or inspiring. They are in alphabetical order; I wouldn't dare rank them.

- Benton and Benton (1990) *Double Vision*: Stimulating teaching and learning.

- Besag (1989) *Bullies and Victims in Schools*: Great understanding shown in this book.

- DES (1989) *Discipline in Schools*: Clear and useful.

- Hargreaves (1982) *The Challenge For The Comprehensive School*: The meaning of schooling.

- Laslett and Smith (1984) *Effective Classroom Management*, or Marland (1975, 1993) *The Craft of the Classroom*: Both books are excellent 'how to do it' guides (I can't decide which one I prefer).

- Macdonald et al. (1989) *Murder in the Playground*: Sensitive, shocking, and unforgettable.

- Oswin (1991) *Am I Allowed to Cry?*: Coping with death, with enormous good sense.

- Redmond and Hush (1980+) *Grange Hill*: A perspective on education understood by pupils.

- Salzberger-Wittenberg, *et al.* (1983) *The Emotional Experience of Learning and Teaching*: Fascinating reflections on teaching.

- Scottish Office and HMI (1992) *Using Ethos Indicators in Secondary School Self-Evaluation*: How to learn about schools.

Books On or Of Research

Favourite 'how to' books are Scottish Office and HMI (1992) *Using Ethos Indicators in Secondary School Self-Evaluation* and Strauss and Corbin (1990) *Basics of Qualitative Research.* The first is especially good on quantitative research, using questionnaires; the second is the best guide to qualitative research. Bell (1987) *Doing Your Research Project:* is comprehensive.

My favourite examples of research are DES (1989) *Discipline in Schools* and Macdonald *et al.* (1989) *Murder in the Playground.* The National Commission on Education's *Briefings for the Paul Hamlyn Foundation National Commission on Education* (1993) is one of the best collections of recent research into key education issues. Walford (1991) *Doing Educational Research* is one of the best accounts of the practical problems met by researchers.

The Teacher in the Classroom

General books on teaching techniques include Laslett and Smith (1984) *Effective Classroom Management* and Marland (1975, 1993) *The Craft of the Classroom.* Peter (1992) *Differentiation: Ways Forward* is good on practicalities; and Salzberger-Wittenberg *et al.* (1983) *The Emotional Experience of Learning and Teaching* is excellent on the psychology of teaching. NCC (1991) *Teaching Talking and Learning in Key Stage Three* and National Oracy Project (1991) *Assessment Through Talk in Key Stages 3 and 4: Occasional Papers in Oracy No. 4,* are both good on oral work.

On equal opportunities, issues of race and ethnicity are covered by Macdonald *et al.*(1989) *Murder in the Playground,* National Union of Teachers (1983) *Combating Racism in Schools,* and Gaine (1988) *No Problem Here.* There are many good books on gender issues, including

Spender (1982) *Invisible Women* Whyte *et al.* (1985) *Girl Friendly Schooling,* and Griffin (1985) *Typical Girls?* On class, Willis (1977) *Learning to Labour* gives an interesting account.

There are many good books on Special Educational Needs, including the important Committee of Enquiry into the Education of Handicapped Children and Young People (chaired by Warnock) (1978) *Special Educational Needs,* and the more recent Department for Education, Welsh Office (1994) *Code of Practice on the Identification and Assessment of Special Educational Needs.* Widlake (1989) *Special Children Handbook* is a good practical account. Bargh (1987) *Play Back the Thinking Memories* is written by pupils with special needs, and so is especially interesting.

Homework, too little studied, I think, is best described by MacBeath and Turner (1990) *Learning Out of School.* It is interesting to compare two government reports, separated by 50 years, but coming to much the same conclusions: Great Britain Board of Education (1936) *Homework: Board of Education Educational Pamphlets, No. 110,* and the Department of Education and Science (DES, 1987) *Education Observed 4.*

Behaviour is covered by Department of Education and Science (1989) *Discipline in Schools* (the Elton Report), and, on the single issue of bullying, by Besag (1989) *Bullies and Victims in Schools.*

Controversial issues are well covered by Dufour (1990) *The New Social Curriculum,* Carrington and Troyna (1988) *Children and Controversial Issues* and Wellington (1986) *Controversial Issues in the Curriculum.*

The Teacher Outside the Classroom

On national policies, Acts of Parliament are of course useful; for an historical account, try Gordon *et al.* (1991) *Education and Policy in England in the Twentieth Century.* On prospective future policies, the best account is probably the National Commission on Education (1993) *Learning to Succeed.*

Management books are never in short supply. Frase (1992) *Maximizing People Power in Schools* and Goodchild and Holly (1989) *Management for Change* are useful, practical, books. Beare *et al.*(1989) *Creating an Excellent School* is good on theories of management, while Roberts (1989) *Leadership Secrets of Attila the Hun* is a constantly fascinating and endlessly applicable book. On middle management, there's Marland (1971) *Head of Department.* Two books with a more psychological approach are Newton and Tarrant (1992) *Managing Change in Schools* and Wehlage *et al.* (1989) *Reducing the Risk.*

Fewer books are written on display. I like Hodgson (1988) *Classroom Display*.

On pupils growing up, primary schooling is well covered by Cockburn (1992) *Beginning Teaching* and Dean (1983, 1991) *Organising Learning in the Primary School Classroom*. The Plowden Report (Central Advisory Council for Education, 1967) is still relevant. On secondary schools, Rutter *et al.* (1979) *Fifteen Thousand Hours* is one of the most famous books, and Willis (1977) *Learning to Labour* is both important and entertaining. Chitty (1990) *Post-16 Education* covers older pupils.

Becoming adult, staying in control, and maintaining self-esteem are covered by many academic and popular psychology books. Berne (1968) *Games People Play* is the classic text of Transactional Analysis. My favourite book on self-esteem is Burns (1982) *Self-Concept Development and Education*. The whole psychology of teaching is interestingly described by Salzberger-Wittenberg *et al.* (1983) *The Emotional Experience of Learning and Teaching*.

Legal and professional matters are described in many leaflets available from teaching unions. Spackman (1991) *Teachers' Professional Responsibilities* is a good general account.

CHAPTER 15

A Personal Annotated Bibliography

This is a bibliography, containing my notes on some of the books I've read (or at least looked at). As I say in the Introduction, the comments here are purely personal, and are not intended to be any weighty academic judgements. Do use this bibliography in whatever way you feel suits your purpose. You may want to look up specific authors, you may be interested in a particular topic; you may be looking for something – anything – interesting to research, or you may be researching for a job interview (did that job application mention flexible learning?).

No doubt some people will look through this list, spotting the missing books. As I started compiling this bibliography, I was aware of how many important books I hadn't read, but I hoped still to read them. However, my reading felt just as incomplete at the end as at the start of my work. I realised that there is no such thing as a definitive list of the 10 (or 100, or 1,000) most important books on education. Don't therefore assume that absence from this list is an indication that a book is not worth reading: it simply means I've not yet read it, or forgotten what it said if I read it a long time ago.

A

Adelman, C. (ed.) (1981) *Uttering, Muttering: Collecting, Using and Reporting Talk for Social and Educational Research*. London: Grant McIntyre.

> P. Woods – *Understanding through Talk* – listening can itself *legitimate* what is said (e.g. smoking or teacher-baiting). Themes in talk – boredom, having a laugh, being shown up, etc. Some enquiries may be "cruel, but true" – so that as an ethnographer "a streak of sadism can, at times, be a useful attribute" (p. 24).

> P. Atkinson – *Inspecting Classroom Talk* – talk so familiar, researcher needs to *make* everyday life "anthropologically strange" (p. 100).

G. Thomas Fox, Jr. – *Pictures of a Thousand Words: Using Graphics in Classroom Interviews* – using coloured pens, etc., not words.

Advisory Committee on Police in Schools (1986) *Policing Schools*. London: Advisory Committee on Police in Schools.

Critical analysis of police 'hearts and minds' campaign in schools. Written just after the Police and Criminal Evidence Act was passed. Interesting technical information, should issues arise in school, and a good example of the controversial nature of apparently uncontroversial events in school.

Ainscow, M. and Florek, A. (eds) (1989) *Special Educational Needs: Towards a Whole School Approach*. London: David Fulton and NCSE.

Clear professional account, centred on means of support – for pupils and teachers – and whole-school policies.

Aldrich, R. (1989) *A Common Countenance: National Curriculum and Testing in England and Wales*. Vancouver: Centre for Policy Studies in Education.

Arends, R. I. (1988, 2nd edn., 1991) *Learning to Teach*. New York: McGraw-Hill.

Very American and very detailed guide for training/beginning teachers, with *lots* on research, plenty on the meaning of teaching, guides to planning, social issues affecting schooling, and classroom skills (very widely defined). The only book I've seen, other than mine, which covers 'how to find out' in similar detail to 'how to teach'. Good for this reason, despite the need for a version adapted for British use.

Association of Assistant Mistresses (1974) *Homework: An AAM Discussion Document*. London: AAM.

Discussion document, including arguments for and against homework – good, clear, if unexciting and (if you've read all the other documents) rather predictable.

B

Banks, O. (1968) *The Sociology of Education*. London: Batsford.

Old-fashioned, academic, thorough text. Interesting, not least, because it gives the impression of representing a (now lost) Anglo-American orthodoxy.

Bargh, J. (compiler) (1987) *Play Back the Thinking Memories;*. London: National Children's Bureau.

Writing by young women (aged 17–20) with moderate learning difficulties. Good writing focused on building self-confidence, and looking like it worked.

Barnes, D., Britton, J. and Torbe, M. (1990) *Language, the Learner and the School;* 4th edn. Portsmouth, NH: Heinemann.

Douglas Barnes always writes well and with enthusiasm.

Barnes, R. (1987) *Teaching Art to Young Children 4–9*. London: Unwin Hyman.

Lively, open-ended, book, encouraging ideas rather than giving lists of 'good' themes – though it does that as well. Good cross-curricular stuff, and many ideas applicable to secondary school too.

Barnet College of Further Education (1978, 1980) *FlexiStudy: A Manual for Local Colleges*. Cambridge: National Extension College Reports, Series 2 Number 4.

Model for really flexible learning. Now a little dated.

Barthorpe, T. and Visser, J. (1991) *Differentiation: Your Responsibility: An In-Service Training Pack for Staff Development*. Stafford: NARE Publications.

Plenty of OHP masters, after a punchy one-page intro, referring to Warnock ('The purpose of education for all children is the same; the goals are the same. But the help that individual children need in progressing towards them will be different.'), and National Curriculum Council (1989; *Curriculum Guidance 2: A Curriculum for All*. York: NCC – i.e. pupils are entitled to a broad balanced and differentiated curriculum relevant to their needs).

Bates, I., Clarke, J., Cohen, P., Finn, D., Moore, R. and Willis, P. (1984) *Schooling for the Dole?: The New Vocationalism*. London: Macmillan.

Very detailed critique, with implications for all teachers.

Beare, H., Caldwell, B. J. and Millikan, R. H. (1989) *Creating an Excellent School: Some New Management Techniques*. London: Routledge.

A good guide to management techniques, concentrating on leadership, culture, structure and accountability, and addressed to Senior Management Teams and others involved in policy-making. New terms like 'entrepreneurship' are being used. Understanding leadership needs more than just a list of 'traits' of 'great men'. The focus should move away from system administration, towards self-determining schools as units in delivery of learning. The essential task of schools is teaching and learning – so schools (should) have an intellectual focus and simple goals, with the goals applying to all. The metaphor used is of student-as-worker, with student exhibitions required (i.e. evidence). Attitudes are clearly important, with 'generalism' being a better quality than 'specialism' for staff to have. Education is personalised learning. The budget demonstrates (or should demonstrate) educational priorities. Leaders should be more transforming (looking to higher aims, motives, changing attitudes, etc.) than transactional (organising current wants, etc.). The school's public image is vital [good advice here!].

Bell, J. (1987, 1993) *Doing Your Research Project: A Guide for First-Time Researchers in Education and Social Science*. Buckingham: Open

University Press.

A comprehensive blow-by-blow account, written for the very reliable Open University. It covers all stages of research, including planning, primary and secondary research techniques, methods of statistical analysis, and the presentation of findings. Lots of examples are given. The book gives so much detail that those who have done very little previous enquiry-based study may at first find it daunting. However, the meaning and significance of each section will become clearer as you progress through your own research. A book worth skimming through regularly, rather than reading at a single sitting at the start of a course.

Bell, J., *et al.* (eds) (1984) *Conducting Small-Scale Investigations in Educational Management.* London: Paul Chapman Publishing in association with The Open University.

Case studies, keeping diaries, interviews and questionnaires, etc. Useful. Detailed.

Bellaby, P. (1977) *The Sociology of Comprehensive Schooling.* London: Methuen.

Analysis of comprehensives in their political/economic contexts. Rather pessimistic – along the lines of 'schools cannot change society' – but allows for 'relative autonomy'. Interesting as representing the break-up of the left–liberal optimism about education reform, which made opposition to the changes of the 1980s much less unified.

Benton, M. and Benton, P. (1990) *Double Vision: Reading Paintings – Reading Poems – Reading Paintings.;* London: Hodder and Stoughton.

Superb book of paintings, and poems written about them (or vice versa), and exercises relating to both. The best example of DARTs work I've seen. Certainly one of the most pleasurable books. Invaluable stimulus for teachers of art, English, History, RE, PSE, and many other subjects; indirectly stimulating for teachers of any subject. The paintings are well chosen and well reproduced, and the poems are good too. This is the sort of book that makes most teachers say 'what an obvious idea – I wish I'd thought of that'. It may be expensive to buy a class set of the books – though I would guess several departments could get together, as it is such a cross-curricular sort of thing – but one copy could at least stimulate the teacher. Copies should be in every school library.

Berne, E. (1968) *Games People Play: The Psychology of Human Relationships.* London: Penguin Books.

Classic text of Transactional Analysis – a way of looking at interactions as games, particularly involving the roles of parent, adult, child. A good, relatively simple, way of analysing what happens in classrooms, avoiding the more scary (and jargon-laden) Freudian analysis. Best used to look for possible gains in apparently damaging activity, e.g. underachievement or misbehaviour.

Besag, V. E. (1989) *Bullies and Victims in Schools.* Milton Keynes: Open University Press.

How to understand/research the issues; what to do about it. Good overview of research, as well as sensitive approach to emotional factors in both bullies and victims, and a good general account of 'popularity' and other emotional factors in learning. Very varied approaches to improving the situation, including general teacher relationships with pupils. Lots of activity/workshop suggestions, as well as case-studies.

Bion, W. R. (1961) *Experiences in Groups and Other Papers*. London: Tavistock Publications.

Psychoanalyst out of Melanie Klein, interested amongst many other things in groups and in (the presence or absence of) the ability to learn from experience. Good group spirit associated with:

'(a) A common purpose, whether that be overcoming an enemy or defending and fostering an ideal or a creative construction in the field of social relationships or in physical amenities. (b) Common recognition by members of the group of the "boundaries" of the group and their position and function in relation to those of larger units or groups. (c) The capacity to absorb new members, and to lose members without fear of losing group individuality – i.e. "group character" must be flexible. (d) Freedom from internal sub-groups having rigid (i.e. exclusive) boundaries. If a sub-group is present it must not be centred on any of its members nor on itself – treating other members of the main group as if they did not belong within the main goup barrier – and the value of the sub-group to the function of the main group must be generally recognized. (e) Each individual member is valued for his contribution to the group and has free movement within it, his freedom of locomotion being limited only by the generally accepted conditions devised and imposed by the group. (f) The group must have the capacity to face discontent within the group and must have means to cope with discontent. (g) The minimum size of the group is three. Two members have personal relationships; with three or more there is a change of quality (interpersonal relationship)' (pp. 25–26).

Biott, C. (1991) *Semi-Detached Teachers: Building Support and Advisory Relationships in Classrooms*. London: Falmer.

A guide to developing collaborative partnerships. Chapter 10, on Advisory Teachers and School Development, quotes Joyce:

'there are three types of school: (1) The Self-Activating School – with a free strong interchange of ideas, considerable energy expended on self development, and warm interchanges fostering growth. Change efforts are supported by strong formal systems, INSET caters for institutional and individual needs, and effective use is made of advisory support. (2) The Comfort School – 'has a semi-positive orientation to change, but efforts are fragmented rather than collective. It is described as 'supportive but not synergistic'.' (3) The Survival School – which has a negative environment, working against change. Individual staff are covert about their personal efforts. Staff feel isolated, and exhibit phobic reactions to possible change.'

Biott, C. and Storey, J. (eds) (1986) *The Inside Story: Initiating and Sustaining Action Research in Schools With External Support*. Cambridge: Cambridge Institute of Education.

Concentrating on self-review/evaluation, especially in Primary schools.

Birch, D. W. and Latcham, J. (1984) *Flexible Learning in Action: Three*

Case Studies of Flexibility. London: Further Education Unit.

> Clear report on three FE college schemes.

Black, H., Blair, A., Malcolm, H., Latta, J. and Zaklukiewicz, S. (1991) *A Whole-School Approach to Resource-Based Learning: A Regional Case Study.* Edinburgh: Scottish Council for Research in Education.

> Excellent report, incorporating results from a model survey – looking at the perspectives of teachers and pupils, and comparing these with the (observed) reality. Student-centred learning has (under different titles) been promoted for so long, it is interesting to see how teachers in the 1980s/1990s are doing. This report is good for anyone looking at or hoping to do effective school-based research, as well as anyone looking at flexible learning.

Blatchford, P. (1989) *Playtime in the Primary School: Problems and Improvements.* Windsor: NFER-Nelson.

> Good 'pupil-eye' view of under-explored issue in Primary schools – which could be applied to Secondary schools, too. Good example of how to tackle/manage a set of 'problems' without obvious solutions; good ideas on topic work (perhaps in PSE?), and on management of the *whole* school workforce.

Blatchford, P. and Sharp, S. (eds) (1994) *Breaktime and the School: Understanding and Changing Playground Behaviour.* London: Routledge.

> Review of research – including aggression, sexism, racism, games, etc. Recent initiatives on school ground design and improvements, management, supervisions, involvement of pupils, whole-school approaches. Primary and secondary schools covered.

Brandes, D. and Phillips, H. (1978) *Gamesters' Handbook: 140 Games for Teachers and Group Leaders.* London: Hutchinson. Also Brandes, D. (1982) *Gamesters' Handbook Two: More Games for Teachers and Group Leaders.* London: Hutchinson.

> Endless ideas for activities (e.g. pin the name of a famous person on each pupil's back, and get them to work out who they are), many of which could be used by confident teachers – pupils would probably become cynical about them if the teacher showed the slightest scepticism.

Buckland, D. and Short, M. (1993) *Nightshift: Ideas and Strategies for Homework.* London: Centre for Information on Language Teaching and Research.

> An interesting brief (40 page) practical guide to setting Modern Languages homework, including ideas applicable to other subjects.

Burgess, R. G. (ed.) (1985) *Field Methods in the Study of Education.* London: Falmer.

R. G. Burgess – *The Whole Truth?: Some Ethical Problems of Research in a Comprehensive School.* About teacher-versus-visitor perspective in research, etc.

R. Walker and J. Wiedel – *Using Photographs in a Discipline of Words* – doing a sequence of photos (e.g. 23 over 10 minutes, of a teacher's desk) – has a "can-opener" effect in bringing out comments' (p. 212).

Burns, R. (1982) *Self-Concept Development and Education.* Eastbourne. Holt, Rinehart and Winston.

Heavyweight, American-style (though British), psychological text, but designed for initial teacher training and INSET. Covers everything, including definitions of self-concept, developmental features, body/appearance, parents, adolescence, significant others, teachers' self-concept (useful), school organisation, prejudice, delinquency. Also, how to enhance pupil self-concept, covering counselling, and teaching approaches – such as making pupils feel supported, responsible, competent, etc., setting realistic goals, realistic self-evaluation and self-praise. Useful exercises scattered through 441 pages.

Byrne, B. (1994) *Coping With Bullying in Schools.* London: Cassell.

Good, clear, guide, including case studies (and that Adrian Mitchell poem, again!).

C

Cambridge Institute of Education (1989) *Thinking Schools: Supporting Schools in Their Staff Development.*; Cambridge: Cambridge Institute of Education, for the Support for Innovation Project.

Staff and school development from inside and outside the school – e.g. *via* the INSET co-ordinator, the school's development committee, the LEA, staff conferences, etc. Communication and feedback and central to overcoming obstacles. Paired observation by teachers is helpful, so that they can share their classroom experiences.

Carrington, B. and Troyna, B. (eds) (1988) *Children and Controversial Issues: Strategies for the Early and Middle Years of Schooling.* London: Falmer.

Fearful of the effects of the Education Reform Act in squeezing out controversial issues from the curriculum, the book is particularly keen to demonstrate the sophisticated discourse on controversial issues demonstrated by young children. For example:

'Jeffcoate exploded the myth by showing that 4-year-olds can not only discriminate racial differences but can also express racially abusive remarks. When the children were initially asked by their teacher to discuss pictures portraying black people in a "variety of situations and in a respectful and unstereotyped way", the children's responses could not possibly be construed as racially offensive. However, when the same set of pictures were left "casually" around the room (but in locations close to concealed tape-recorders), the comments made by the children, in the assumed absence of an adult audience, were undeniably racist in tenor. Although this study confirmed the results of previous research into the early onset of anti-black sentiment in white children, it is, perhaps, more important in showing that, even at the nursery stage, children are cognisant of the socially unacceptable nature of these feelings and of the need to conceal them in the presence of adult authority' (p. 21).

As well as general issues to do with the status and role of the teacher, there are chapters on specific issues – the world of work, sexism, race and conflict, sexuality, and racism.

Cartwright, F. F. (1972) *Disease and History.* London: Hart-Davis, MacGibbon.

An account of various ways in which history may have been affected by disease. For connoisseurs of trivia, though it is a terribly serious topic, of course.

Castles, S. and Wüstenberg, W. (1979) *The Education of the Future: An Introduction to the Theory and Practice of Socialist Education.* London: Pluto Press.

Optimistic after-the-revolution approach, looking at history (Owen, Marx) and current 'polytechnic' (in the original sense) practice in the USSR, East Germany, China, and schools like the Tvind and Freinet schools. Happily open-minded.

Central Advisory Council for Education (England) (chaired by Lady Plowden) (1967) *Children and Their Primary Schools, Vol. 1: The Report.* London: HMSO.

Most famous report on primary education, covering child development, the environment and family and its influence, health and social services, nursery provision, organisation of primary education (including links with environment and with other stages of schooling), primary curriculum (and an interesting note of reservation on religious education), staff and training, buildings and equipment. Parodied by the government and press 20 years later as recommending 'caring' education.

Chisholm, J. and Twilley, R. (eds) (1977) *Homework: A Guide for Parents of Primary School Children.* Horsham: Artemis.

By now, rather old-fashioned book (given changes in the curriculum), starting with reading/writing. Practical guide, mostly for parallel work to be done by parents. Of historical interest, particularly.

Chitty, C. (1989) *Towards a New Education System: The Victory of the New Right?* London: Falmer.

An analysis of recent changes, especially in secondary education in England and Wales, with the background of the virtual abolition of local government power – and the consequent change in the 'triangle of tension' between central government, local government, and the individual school. The 'New Right' managed a reversal of the 'left-wing ratchet' (Joseph) in education, and was led by the Centre for Policy Studies (1974, Joseph, Thatcher, Alfred Sherman) and the Conservative Philosophy Group (1975, Scruton, John Casey). Callaghan's 1976 Ruskin speech was a response to economic crisis and falling rolls. Callaghan presented himself as a lay person, daring to criticise the 'experts'. This book is a good, full, history – from 1944 to the late 1980s.

Chitty, C. (1990) *Post-16 Education: Studies in Access and Achievement.* London: Kogan Page.

Self-explanatory title!

Chitty, C. (1992) *The Education System Transformed: A Guide to the School Reforms.* Manchester: Baseline.

Clay, M. M. (1972) *Reading: The Patterning of Complex Behaviour.* London: Heinemann Educational Books.

Very clear analysis, with plenty of examples/illustrations, based on studies of 5 to 8 year-olds in New Zealand. Pragmatic, problem-solving approach.

Cockburn, A. D. (1992) *Beginning Teaching: An Introduction to Early Years Education.* London: Paul Chapman.

For prospective teachers of 4–8 year-olds. Very good at giving both atmosphere and information, on children and schools. The primary school background means that child-centredness, rather than focus on academic subjects, is enormously strong. A good lesson, therefore, for prospective (and practising) secondary teachers, too.

Cohen, A. and Cohen L. (eds) (1986) *Special Educational Needs in the Ordinary School.* A Sourcebook for Teachers; London: Harper and Row.

Quite tough, critical, approach to the implications of the 1981 Act. A lot on social, economic and political issues that would need to be tackled alongside integration.

Committee of Enquiry into the Education of Handicapped Children and Young People (chaired by Mrs H. M. Warnock) (1978) *Special Educational Needs.* London: HMSO.

Dominant work on Special Educational Needs – defining the terms and stimulating the 1981 Education Act, which follows it admiringly. Never disagreed with but much undermined, mainly for economic reasons – the integration at the heart of the Report might cost too much. The committee's terms of reference covered 'children and young people handicapped by disabilities of body or mind', which they interpreted broadly to cover emotional and behavioural issues, but not so broadly as to include 'gifted' children. Children with SEN were for the first (official) time given one unifying 'definition' that could easily be applied to a wide range of reasons for having special needs. It said that 20% – one in five – of all children would have SEN at some (or every) stage in their school careers (and one in six children at any one time), and this huge proportion of pupils would of necessity have their needs met mainly in ordinary schools. Needs were seen as of three possible types: needs for the provision of special means of access to the curriculum; needs for the provision of a special or modified curriculum; and needs for particular attention to the social structure and emotional climate in which education takes place. There should be clear stages of assessment of need. Warnock identified five stages (*see* DFE Welsh Office, 1994), the first three being in school, then by a multi-professional team, who might, where appropriate, produce a form that identifies the individual child's needs. (The 1981 Act enshrined the assessment into a 'Statement of Special Educational Needs' – hence children may be referred to as being 'statemented' or as having a 'statement'.) The Warnock Report is a model of what such a report should say, though it isn't especially interesting to read as a text.

Since the Report was published, and in the 1990s in particular, Baroness Warnock has described some of the problems with the Report – in particular, with the financing of support for those pupils with Special Educational Needs who are *not* statemented. She is quoted (in *Special Children,* No.61, November/December 1992) as saying the Report was 'naive to the point of idiocy'.

'There is evidence now that the system never worked as we hoped – and that it could not have done so....The idea of a continuum of ability and disability, with those only at the very end identified by a "statement" was too vague. It was all very well as an ideal....But as a basis for legislation, especially at a time when LEAs were increasingly short of money, it was disastrous.'

Cordingley, P. and Kogan, M. (1993) *In Support of Education: Governing the Reformed System.* London: Jessica Kingsley.

Research into the various actual and possible ways in which central and local government manage education.

Cyngor Defnyddwyr Cymru (1985) *WCC's response to 'Homework' – A Consultation Paper from the Department of Education and Science. See* Welsh Consumer Council (1985).

D

D'Albert, M. (1989) *Medical Matters.* London: DCLD Publications; later published with author unnamed by SENJIT at the Institute of Education.

Brief (49 page) but extremely thorough guide to most common medical conditions which children are likely to have, from the very common (like eczema) to the less common (like cystic fibrosis). After an introduction to the condition, there is a guide to its educational implications – including any associated learning difficulties (either as a result of the condition or of the medication used to control it), how the condition is to be managed in school, and (unusually for such a book) the implications for the emotional development of the child. Precisely as much medical information as a teacher might require, along with very useful, practical, guide to the educational implications of each condition. Written by the Deputy Head of a Special School for Delicate Children – originally a TB school, then for those with specific medical conditions, and now, increasingly, for children who might be called 'emotionally' delicate.

Dale, P., *et al.* (1986) *Dangerous Families: Assessment and Treatment of Child Abuse.* London: Tavistock.

Full account of assessment and (mainly therapeutic) treatment, based on and written by the NSPCC. Graphic; scary. Perhaps most useful, for teachers, as a guide to limit amateurish interference (where a teacher suspects that a pupil has been abused) and to promote referral in appropriate circumstances to agencies who can do excellent work.

Dale, R., Fergusson, R., and Robinson, A. (eds) (1988) *Frameworks for*

Teaching: Readings for the Intending Secondary Teacher. London: Hodder and Stoughton/Open University.

27 varied articles, working outwards from the classroom to the school to the social framework. Heavyweights (like Fish on Special Educational Needs, and Bernstein on education not compensating for society) abound, but the editors make sure that a very wide variety of issues relevant to the 1980s (and beyond) are covered. No stone left unturned. Not intended as an 'easy read': most of the articles need to be worked with.

Dalin, P. and Rust, V. D. (1983) *Can Schools Learn?* Windsor: NFER-Nelson.

Per Dalin is head of IMTEC – International Movements Towards Educational Change (out of OECD). A study of the mutuality of an institution's creativity and its adaptation processes (including openness to outside influences). It is not good if either is low.

Daniels, H. and Ware, J. (eds) (1990) *Special Educational Needs and the National Curriculum: The Impact of the Education Reform Act.* London: Kogan Page/Institute of Education, University of London.

Brief (68 page) and broadly pessimistic account of some key issues, including curricular and financial issues.

Davies, B., Ellison, L., Osborne, A. and West-Burnham, J. (1991) *Education Management for the 1990s.* Harlow: Longman.

Well-known introduction to key issues.

Davis, A. M., Williams, G. A. E., Robertson, D. and Pitt, M. (1989) *Health and Safety: A Guide for Staff in Higher Education.* London: Committee of Directors of Polytechnics.

A guide to the Health and Safety Act 1974 – including implications for corporate institutions. Many vital issues are covered. Fire (including fire marshals, and fire drills); environmental health; health of employees. Staff should set an example to students. There should be a suitably qualified safety officer (with wide-ranging access, etc.); there should be safety representatives (e.g. from unions). The institution has a duty to set up procedures *and* to enforce them – including if necessary by dismissal. Staff not complying may (also) be guilty of criminal offence as having 'failed to co-operate'. The institution has a 'duty of care' to visitors, and it therefore may need a range of (reasonable) disclaimers – on e.g. bookings, publications, car parks, personal belongings, etc. Licences are needed, e.g. for petrol, explosives, entertainment, liquor, and firearms. Noise, lighting, VDUs, and catering may all have health and safety implications. Other issues include First Aid, smoking, alcoholism, and AIDS. There is a question and answer section. For example, what is the responsibility of Heads of Department? (To ensure safe working practices, appoint a member of staff with that responsibility, prepare a departmental Safety Handbook.) There is a model Health and Safety Policy – including training, and a model list of duties of the safety and fire officers.

Dean, J. (1983, 1991) *Organising Learning in the Primary School Classroom.* London: Routledge.

A sound, detailed, book on primary practice. Lots on just about everything, including non-judgemental analysis of your own organisational practices (good for all teachers); sensitive, flexible, work on child development; motivation; effective schooling; analysis of teaching styles and strategies; the curriculum; learning difficulties; parents; assessment and record-keeping.

Dearing, R. (1993) *The National Curriculum and its Assessment: An Interim Report.* York: NCC.

Panicked over in the Summer/Autumn of 1993, until the Final Report came out in December. Worth looking at to see what was left out of or changed for the Final Report.

Dearing, R. (1993) *The National Curriculum and its Assessment: Final Report.* London: SCAA.

Proposals for a revision of the National Curriculum. Produced on the recommendation of what was reported as a panicking Secretary of State; generally welcomed as a 'common sense' look at the National Curriculum, done by someone who seemed to value the views of professionals; since being published, rather less enthusiastically welcomed. Some of the problems come from what might be called 'vested interests' – e.g. History teachers worried that History could well be kicked out of Key Stage 4 by many schools. Some come from those who welcomed some of the prescription of the 'old' National Curriculum, seeing it as establishing pupils' rights to a broad and balanced curriculum – especially when Dearing seemed to allow for (even recommend) an apparent academic/vocational split at Key Stage 4. Some come from the fact that, despite its title, the report recommends widespread revision of subject orders, to be done by SCAA, which is expected to open all sorts of cans of worms – e.g. the debate over 'facts' in History. Certainly a well-written, thoughtful, report. It may end up being the National Curriculum's turning point (turning away from prescription) or it may end up just being evidence of pragmatic muddle-through.

DES (Department of Education and Science) (1985) *Homework. Note by the Department of Education and Science.* London: DES.

A discussion paper following on from the *Better Schools* White Paper of 1985.

DES (Department of Education and Science) (1987) *Homework: A Report by HM Inspectors.* London: DES.

A follow-up to the previous discussion document, including a survey and results from 243 schools – though note that it is by definition difficult to measure, and that the survey was done during a teachers' dispute:

'Those schools where homework had greater consistency, purpose and support were generally characterised by the belief that, among the teachers, an effective policy needed to involve not only the senior management team but departmental, pastoral and tutorial staff and be the product of extensive discussion. Moreover the communication of this policy to parents and pupils and, in some cases, the dialogue which this evoked were no less important to the policy's effectiveness than its acceptance by the whole teaching staff.'

'Where homework involves more than routine tasks, it has at least one of the following characteristics: it is closely integrated with and reinforces classwork and has clear curricular objectives; it exploits the materials and resources in the environment and the community outside the school; it encourages independence, research, creativity and initiative; and it promotes the cooperation and involvement of parents and other adults.'

DES (Department of Education and Science) (1989) *Discipline in Schools: Report of the Committee of Enquiry chaired by Lord Elton.* London: HMSO.

Superbly written – clear, non-technical, useful, and concise – report on behaviour in maintained mainstream primary and secondary schools. The committee was set up following press scares about violence against teachers, and what should be done about it. The report, incidentally, comes to the surprising conclusion that even when teachers are involved in violent incidents, they are unlikely to regard these as the most difficult problems to deal with. Rather than looking at school rules (things not to do) it looks at behaviour policies (things to do), and therefore enables teachers, pupils, and others involved in the school to look at positive approaches to behaviour. The separate perspectives and concerns of parents, pupils, teachers, schools (and managements), police, and local/central government are all dealt with. All people concerned with a school should get together to work out appropriate behaviour policies. Several 'Elton Projects' have been set up since the report was published. The report really is a model of how to write a powerful and sensitive guide to good practice.

Devereux, K. (1982) *Understanding Learning Difficulties.* Milton Keynes: Open University Press.

Detailed, psychological, if at times a little technical and cold description of learning processes of children with learning difficulties.

DFE (Department for Education) (1994a) *Religious Education and Collective Worship: Circular Number 1/94.* London: DFE.

Aim of RE (p. 12):

'Religious education in schools should seek: to develop pupils' knowledge, understanding and awareness of Christianity, as the predominant religion in Great Britain, and the other principal religions represented in the country; to encourage respect for those holding different beliefs; and to help promote pupils' spiritual, moral, cultural and mental development.'

Aims of Collective Worship (p. 20):

'Collective worship in schools should aim to provide the opportunity for pupils to worship God, to consider spiritual and moral issues and to explore their own beliefs; to encourage participation and response, whether through active involvement in the presentation of worship or through listening to and joining in the worship offered; and to develop community spirit, promote a common ethos and shared values, and reinforce positive attitudes.'

p. 21:

"Worship" is not defined in the legislation and in the absence of any such definition it should be taken to have its natural and ordinary meaning. That is, it must in some sense reflect something special or separate from ordinary school activities and it should be concerned with reverence or veneration paid to a divine being or power.'

DFE (Department for Education) (1994b) *Pupils With Problems: Pupil Behaviour and Discipline, The Education of Children with Emotional and Behavioural Difficulties, Exclusions from School, The Education by LEAs of Children Otherwise than at School, The Education of Sick Children, The Education of Children Being Looked After by Local Authorities:* London: DFE.

A collection of circulars. Some points: EBD (emotional and behavioural difficulties) forms part of a continuum: 'At one end are children who are naughty, and at the other children and adolescents with mental illnesses. Children with EBD in between.' The document sets out arrangements for 'pupil referral units' (PRUs) in which 'the curriculum should be balanced and broadly based and should promote the spiritual, moral, cultural, mental and physical development of pupils.' Various bits and pieces about behaviour, bullying, assessment procedures, whole-school policies, exchange of information between institutions, appropriate and inappropriate rewards and sanctions, abolition of indefinite exclusions, etc.

DFE (Department for Education), Welsh Office (1994) *Code of Practice on the Identification and Assessment of Special Educational Needs.* London: DFE.

Came into effect September 1994. Revision of 1981 legislation, under the 1993 Education Act (though the code, too, was approved by Parliament). Assessment stages re-done:

'Stage 1: class or subject teachers identify or register a child's special educational needs and, consulting the school's SEN coordinator, take initial action. Stage 2: the school's SEN coordinator takes lead responsibility for gathering information and for coordinating the child's special educational provision, working with the child's teachers. Stage 3: teachers and the SEN coordinator are supported by specialists from outside the school. Stage 4: the LEA consider the need for a statutory assessment and, if appropriate, make a multidisciplinary assessment. Stage 5: the LEA consider the need for a statement of special educational needs and, if appropriate, make a statement and arrange, monitor and review provision.'

Note the implication, highlighted by the NUT and the Spastics Society, of Stage 3, that schools arrange for external support, before the LEA gets involved. As before: SEN as learning difficulty (greater difficulty than peers or disability hindering access to facilities), not difficulty resulting from language/form of language of the home; 20% of pupils have some form of SEN, 2% are likely to require statementing. The increased role of the SEN coordinator (or team) – includes 'responsibility for the day-to-day *operation* of the school's SEN policy and for coordinating provision for pupils with special educational needs, particularly at stages 2 and 3' (p. 7). A lot more on SEN policy, and its implementation. Time limits (recommended) for LEAs and others making statutory assessments and statements: 26 weeks from first giving notice to parents. Examples are given of questions that might be asked of parents.

Dickinson, C. and Wright, J. (1993) *Differentiation: A Practical Handbook of Classroom Strategies.* London: National Council for Educational Technology.

Differentiation by resource, support, task, response, etc.

Donaldson, M. (1978) *Children's Minds*. London: Fontana.

A classic – surprisingly, perhaps, as it is a short (less than 150 pages of text), clear, and largely lacking technical vocabulary. The book, amongst other things, revises some of Piaget's most famous descriptions of the development of thinking in children. For example, Piaget described the development of an understanding of 'conservation' – the stage at which a child would understand that two beakers of water with the same amount of water, would still have the same amount of water when one beaker was poured into a long thin container. Donaldson notes that the experiment itself may give children the idea that something *should* have changed: that is, the thinking of young children might be more sophisticated (and dependent on non-linguistic, social, clues) than Piaget had suggested, and that abstract thinking ('disembedded intellectual activity') is a very distinct skill. The central point of the book, though, is not simply to describe the development of children's minds, but to use the understanding of this development to help improve schools. Why are schools so often such unpleasant places, especially in the later years? 'The experience becomes wretched at present largely because it is a wretched thing to be compelled to do something at which you persistently fail' (p. 124). The skill of 'disembedded intellectual ability' is a difficult one to acquire. Schools may just give up on the task, which may allow for happy play in the early years, but which will many leave older pupils frustrated and awkward. Or schools may recognise the difficulty, and try to overcome it. Donaldson recognises that this is, of course, easier said than done.

Donovan, K. G. (1981) *Learning Resources in Colleges: Their Organization and Management*. London: Council for Educational Technology.

Clear pack, in the style of a training manual, incorporating useful definitions, etc.

Dufour, B. (ed.) (1990) *The New Social Curriculum: A Guide to Cross-Curricular Issues*. Cambridge: Cambridge University Press.

The editor previously co-wrote *The New Social Studies* (Lawton and Dufour, 1973), and this book represents the possibilities of the re-emergence of social studies/humanities teaching, after the National Curriculum. What had often been 'subjects' are now more likely to be 'themes', as a result of political decisions. The areas of study covered by this book include vocational education, PSE, health, media, peace, gender, multicultural and anti-racist, global, environmental, trade union, and human rights education. Each chapter puts the theme in context, and each one ends with very useful lists of references, key teacher and pupil resources, and addresses for further information. It would of course be absurd to take each theme as a new subject to be crammed in to the already crowded curriculum, like some Japanese train guard. (Some reviews of the book took this line, criticising it, strangely, for being too optimistic.) Rather, any or all of the themes could inform practice in any number of ways. An immensely useful book, therefore, for practising teachers, for prospective teachers, and for researchers into one or all of the issues covered.

Dyson, A. and Gains, C. (1993) *Rethinking Special Needs in Mainstream Schools: Towards the Year 2000*. London: David Fulton.

Includes section on using soft systems methodology to rethink Special Needs.

E

Elliott, M. (1990) *Teenscape: A Personal Safety Programme for Teenagers.* London: Health Education Authority.

Excellent, practical, detailed, 'what to do's', and examples of good practice by schools, etc. Also books and further information. Usable by teenagers and adults (including teachers).

Elton Report: *See* DES (1989)

Everard, K. B. and Morris, G. (1990) *Effective School Management,* 2nd edn. London: Paul Chapman.

Detailed and practical.

F

Faraday, A. (1972) *Dream Power: The Use of Dreams in Everyday Life.* London: Pan.

Lovely, flexible, eclectic book on dreaming. *Not* a guide of the type that says 'if you dream of an aubergine, it means your carburettor needs cleaning'. It looks at various different theories, and ways of interpreting dreams, with the reader left to choose whichever suits. One section (in Chapter 11) on the (possible) use of dreams in schools. (See also Faraday (1974) *The Dream Game.* New York: Harper and Row.)

FEU (Further Education Unit) (1983) *Flexible Learning Opportunities.* London: FEU.

Many case studies, with the FEU's commentary following each one – looking at advantages for learners, teachers and managers. It is the case studies that make the booklet most useful:

'Flexible learning is defined...as the creation of learning opportunities tailored to meet the needs of the learner. Components of this concept include learner autonomy and effectiveness, which are dependent in turn on the extent to which the process of learning is matched to the individual learner's needs for employment or otherwise, via negotiation and counselling and guidance'.

FEU (Further Education Unit) (1987) *Quality in NAFE.* London: FEU.

Very detailed, though only 32 pages long, rather tedious booklet on quality. Nevertheless, could be useful.

FEU (Further Education Unit) (1991) *Quality Matters: Business and Industry Quality Models and Further Education.* London: FEU.

'Quality' can be seen as a degree of excellence or as fitness for purpose, arrived at through conformance to specification. The book includes measures of how good a college is, looking at choice, advice, flexibility over what or how to learn, how the curriculum is taught or learned, how ethnic diversity is dealt with, how gender and special needs are addressed, how motivated the staff are, liaison with parents, the community, local schools, business and industry, etc., how entry to and progression from the college is prepared for and supported, what professional, technical and administrative support is available, how effectively all these concerns are managed, and how these all meet learners' needs and expectations. How cost-effective is the college? What reputation and standing does it have in the community? What physical condition is it in? TQM (Total Quality Management) is described – as never being satisfied, aiming for continuous quality improvement. TQM and BS5750 (now known as BS EN ISO 9000) are management models which are not, however, designed for educational establishments. Which, if either, is appropriate 'to improve the quality of teaching and learning, to increase participation, and to improve attainment'? 'The process is predicated on the principle that quality begins and ends with shared commitment, attitude and actions' (p. 3). Detailed analysis of BS5750 (including lots of paperwork) and TQM, including examples of colleges that have tried them. Quality improvement must primarily seek to improve the quality of teaching and learning; it must be flexible; it must harness the commitment of all (teaching and non-teaching) staff; it should involve learners in improving the quality of teaching and learning.

Field, M. (1993) *APL: Developing More Flexible Colleges*. London: Routledge.

APL is the accreditation of prior learning, including experiential learning. It is a vital part of the NVQ developments – recognising experience (or what old cynics used to call 'the university of life', though I'll get shot for mentioning that), and building on students' previous learning. It may seem obvious, but in the past, most post-16 education took little account of previous learning – tending to dismiss school-based learning, for example, as inappropriate. APL is another great, big, idea; though its application at first developed a reputation for being rather bureaucratic. This book is clear enough, with plenty of diagrams.

Finn, D. (1987) *Training Without Jobs: New Deals and Broken Promises: From Raising the School Leaving Age to the Youth Training Scheme*. London: Macmillan Education.

Full, pessimistic, historical account (going back to the beginnings of compulsory schooling) of the development of the 'new vocationalism'. Good on the shift to a new relationship between school, training, and work.

Fontana, D. (1986) *Classroom Control*. Leicester: British Psychological Society.

A Psychologist's approach, clearly written. Looks at causes of problems of class control, including the child, the teacher and the school; looks at how to 'guide and reshape' problematic behaviour. Good on self-image (of all concerned), etc.

Francis, H. (ed.) (1985) *Learning to Teach: Psychology in Teacher Training*. London: Falmer.

A good set of article titles, on the theme of how useful psychology is in teacher training and schools. A fiercely academic, heavyweight, introduction to no doubt useful further work.

Frase, L. E. (1992) *Maximizing People Power in Schools: Motivating and Managing Teachers and Staff.* Newbury Park, CA: Corwin.

> An immensely useful, entertaining, description of effective and ineffective school management (in the USA), with ideas on burnout, observation of teachers, setting goals (including finding out what pupils think of their teachers), and how to help and, if necessary, get rid of incompetent teachers. The philosophy is of practical, assertive, management. A taste of it is given by the advice that managers should as a matter of course give demonstration lessons, so that those whom they manage know what is expected.

Frase, L. and Hetzel, R. (1990) *School Management by Wandering Around.* Lancaster, PA: Technomics.

G

Gaine, C. (1988) *No Problem Here: A Practical Approach to Education and 'Race' in White Schools.* London: Hutchinson.

Gibbs, G. (1981) *Teaching Students to Learn: A Student-Centred Approach.* Milton Keynes: Open University.

> Ex-OU setter-up. Learning, organising, noting, reading, writing, exams. No good just telling students how to learn: structured exercises needed. Good.

Gillham, B. (ed.) (1983) *Reading Through the Curriculum: Proceedings of the Nineteenth Annual Course and Conference of the United Kingdom Reading Association Newcastle upon Tyne Polytechnic, 1982.* London: Heinemann Educational.

> Various articles on language and reading through the curriculum

Gillham, B. (ed.) (1986) *Handicapping Conditions in Children.* London: Croom Helm.

> Clear definitions, provision, implications, etc. (based in the USA) of mental handicap, language disorders, autism, and physical/brain disorders.

Gipps, C. and Stobbart (1993) *Assessment: A Teachers' Guide to the Issues.* London: Hodder and Stoughton.

Glaser, B. G. (1978) *Theoretical Sensitivity: Advances in the Methodology of Grounded Theory.* Mill Valley: Sociology Press.

> Sensitivity in this context involves having few prior hypotheses. Fit is vital – i.e. the categories of the theory must fit the data.

Glaser, B. G. and Strauss, A. L. (1967) *The Discovery of Grounded Theory: Strategies for Qualitative Research.* New York: Aldine.

> How to generate theory – i.e. (roughly) how to build theory on your findings, rather

than looking for findings to fit your theory. Various operations are described for generating theory – including the discovery of important categories and their properties, their conditions and consequences; the development of such categories at different levels of conceptualisations; the formulation of hypotheses of varying scope and generality; and the integration of the total theoretical framework. The comparative method permeates all of sociology. The Sociologist Merton (the 'opposition', as this book sees him) believes in systematic quantitative research, in which theory can usefully be generated through speculation or reformulation of others' speculations:

'His reasoning necessarily leads to the position *that data should fit the theory,* in contrast to our position that *the theory should fit the data.'* 'Why not take the data and develop from them a theory that fits and works, instead of wasting time and good men in attempts to fit a theory based on 'reified' ideas of culture and social structure?' (p. 262).

Goffman, E. (1968) *Stigma: Notes on the Management of Spoiled Identity.* Harmondsworth: Penguin.

Standard, readable, account of stigma, including the relationship of stigma to self-image, group identity, stereotyping, and the 'moral career' of the person. Instantly recognisable behaviours are described and given meanings. Useful way beyond its immediate topic.

Goodchild, S. and Holly, P. (1989) *Management for Change: The Garth Hill Experience.* New York: Falmer.

The first half is a 'how I turned a school around' guide by Goodchild. A vivid description, down to the fine details of cleaning out the toilet block. Dynamic leadership in a time of change, with an emphasis on getting everyone (pupils, parents, staff, etc.) involved in the implementation of broad aims as well as practical details. Aims of school set at staff 'conference', which included principles of 'organisational health' – agreed objectives/plans, decisions made close to the problems, SMT responsible for growth of their 'subordinates', communication 'relatively open and trusting', discussion over tasks not arguments over personalities, management ethos of helping *all* to maintain integrity and uniqueness and full member of team, built-in self-criticism at staff meetings, etc., continuous re-examination of bureaucracy. The 'learning school' – maximise the learning of pupils, accept the importance of the learning of teachers, teachers learning together for the development of the school, the school must 'learn its way forward'.

Gordon, P. Aldrich, R. and Dean, D. (1991) *Education and Policy in England in the Twentieth Century.* London: Woburn.

Great Britain Board of Education (1936) *Homework (Educational Pamphlets, No. 110).* London: HMSO.

Astonishingly similar report to those done half a century later (DES, 1985, 1987) – including the interesting comparisons of primary and secondary, the disparity between amount of homework perceived by teachers and by pupils, and variation in practice between schools. Based on surveys done from 1935. An example of home conditions:

'Except in a few cases the children return home to work in the common living room.

Often a meal is in more or less continuous session, the wireless booms and the family chatters. Against such odds, work which might be completed comfortably in a short school period may linger fitfully throughout the evening'.

Estimates of time spent on homework varied from a few minutes a night to over 3 hours a night; 30–40 minutes was the commonest estimate, but 1½ hours was not uncommon. Parents can or should be involved, especially for younger children. Again, half a century before the Strathclyde 'pilots', reference is made to 'homework classes', 'established by one Local Education Authority in certain of its poor districts'.

Griffin, C. (1985) *Typical Girls?: Young Women From School to the Job Market.* London: Routledge and Kogan Paul.

Essential description of the final year at school (in the late 1970s), and first year after school, of young women in Birmingham. Very lively and readable, and should be embarrassing for anyone who has any single picture of a 'typical' girl. The author appreciates complexities without fence-sitting. A model of research, and a vital starting point for any study of gender and sexuality.

Gross, R. D. (1987) *Psychology: The Science of Mind and Behaviour.* London: Hodder and Stoughton.

Clear and full basic text, designed for A Level, but very useful beyond. Most useful chapters for teachers include those on learning, self-concept, adolescence, and intelligence. Non-dogmatic, but doesn't avoid controversy. (Measurement of development, intelligence, etc., has become even more important with the introduction of the National Curriculum's assessment and reporting schemes.)

Gross, R D (1990) *Key Studies in Psychology.* London: Hodder and Stoughton.

Companion to Gross (1987). Useful abridged original studies, for example Milgram (Chapter 10) on obedience (people are surprisingly and dangerously obedient), and Rosenhan (Chapter 29) on being sane in insane places (good on the power of prejudice over observation), etc.

H

Hahn, J. (1985) *'Have You Done Your Homework?': A Parent's Guide to Helping Teenagers Succeed in School.* New York: John Wiley and Sons.

An American guide including some useful bits, such as work on time management, on research ('term papers'), and on appropriate attitudes of parents to their children's (home)work.

Hall, S. and Jefferson, T. (eds) (1975, 1976) *Resistance Through Rituals: Youth Subcultures in Post-war Britain.* London: Hutchinson.

Although the subcultures themselves may be old-fashioned (Teds, Mods, Skinheads, etc.), the analysis is still useful. The theory is of subcultures as responses to social/economic/class positions (i.e. 'strategies for negotiating concrete collective existence'), with clear cultural origins. Good descriptions, too, of moral panics, and other forms of public/media response. One (only one) chapter on girls and subcultures (by McRobbie and Garber), which is important.

Hamblin, D. (1983) *Guidance: 16–19*. Oxford: Blackwell.

A guide to tutoring, aimed at FE Colleges. Full of useful case studies of student–teacher talk, and ideas for problem-solving activities related to social, academic and work skills.

Hanko, G. (1985) *Special Needs in Ordinary Classrooms: An Approach to Teacher Support and Pupil Care in Primary and Secondary Schools.* Oxford: Basil Blackwell.

Case-study-based, clearly and practically focused work mainly on emotional/ behavioural problems of children, and the support needed by their teachers. Lots of material that could be used for INSET, although primarily management-focused in its recommendations.

Hargreaves, D. H. (1972) *Interpersonal Relations and Education.* London: Routledge and Kegan Paul.

Broadly psychological guide, written by someone now better known as a sociologist, to the theory of classroom interactions, and the application of theory to practical situations. A bit heavy at times, but essentially straightforward, with good characterisations of types of roles taken on by pupils and teachers. For example, three types of teacher are described: the Liontamers, the Entertainers (perhaps like Marland or Laslett), and the New Romantics (basically Rogerian). Plenty of good case-studies, though they seem a bit old fashioned now.

Hargreaves, D. H. (1982) *The Challenge For The Comprehensive School: Culture, Curriculum and Community.* London: Routledge and Kegan Paul.

Standard teacher-training and sociology text, written after the author had published many other books on the sociology of schools, concentrating on interaction in schools – behaviour, status, etc. An approach that remains popular because it allowed for practical improvements in schools covering most of the perceived problems. Starts with a wonderful description of the indignities of the hidden curriculum. Chapter 6 (`a proposal and some objections') is a sort of manifesto for positive thinking about comprehensive schooling. The descriptions of school are similar in some ways to Paul Willis, but without the relatively pessimistic (at least in the short-term) Marxist economic foundation. Hargreaves went on to work for ILEA, as chief inspector, and is therefore particularly useful as someone quite prepared to 'put his money where his mouth is'.

Hargreaves, D. H. (1984) *Improving Secondary Schools. See* ILEA (1984).

Harré, R. and Lamb, R. (eds) (1986) *The Dictionary of Developmental and Educational Psychology.* Oxford: Blackwell.

Much fuller accounts than you might expect. Good, clear, wide-ranging, and with

146

plenty of references to key primary texts.

Hegarty, S., Pocklington, K. and Lucas, D. (1981) *Educating Pupils with Special Needs in the Ordinary School.* Windsor: NFER-Nelson.

Very detailed (555 page) account of the integration of pupils with physical, sight and hearing impairment, including historical and international contexts.

Hodgson, A., Clunies-Ross, L. and Hegarty, S. (1984) *Learning Together: Teaching Pupils with Special Educational Needs in the Ordinary School.* Windsor: NFER-Nelson.

Quite clear, organisationally/management-focused, work about physical, sight and hearing impairment. Useful final chapter of guidelines for classroom practice.

Hodgson, N. (1988) *Classroom Display: Improving the Visual Environment in Schools.* Diss: Tarquin.

Very clear, very fully illustrated, thorough guide to display from the smallest scale (how to produce an effective invitation) to the largest (how to put on a major exhibition). Examples from primary and secondary schools. Practical advice on, for example, lettering, layout and binding, as well as broader advice on raising the school's profile in the community.

Holt, J. (1969) *How Children Fail.* Harmondsworth: Penguin.

A book that changed the way people thought about school. Failure is not to do with lack of intelligence or skill, but, often, fear. Fear of embarrassment, fear of failure, fear, perhaps, even of success. A lesson for 'nice' teachers – who may create just as much fear as 'nasty' teachers more obviously do. If pupils can't feel secure enough to learn from their failures, they will learn very little. (The same, of course, can be said of teachers.)

Holt, J. (1984) *How Children Learn.* Harmondsworth: Penguin.

Companion to the author's *How Children Fail.* His approach is now so well known that it is easy to think it is obvious: don't pre-judge children, but observe them and come to understand and respect their own interpretations of what is going on in the classroom. The book looks in detail at talk, reading, sport, art, maths, and a few other areas of development of young children.

Hopkins, D. and Wideen, M. (eds) (1984) *Alternative Perspectives on School Improvement.* London: Falmer.

How to create 'the autonomous school', by, for example, introducing innovation to pupils (i.e. get them involved!).

I

ILEA (1984) *Improving Secondary Schools: Report of the Committee on the Curriculum and Organisation of Secondary Schools.* London: ILEA.

Known as the Hargreaves Report. Solid, very practical, report. All kinds of ways suggested on analysing and improving education, including overcoming disadvantages deriving from social class, etc.

ILEA (1985) *Educational Opportunities for All?: Report of the Committee Reviewing Provision to Meet Special Educational Needs;*. London: ILEA. (The Fish Report.)

Fish, along the way, usefully summarises Warnock and the 1981 Act, and gives examples of good/interesting practice around ILEA. The report, though, has been perceived as the key 'integrationist' report – arguing that most provision for pupils with SEN can or should be provided in mainstream schools. (If you read the report, you'll find that it isn't as simple as that, of course!) Integration has tremendous implications for resourcing. As you might expect, especially since the death of ILEA, the pressure to integrate (and close down Special Schools) has not been matched by sufficient resourcing for mainstream schools. Oh well.

Illich, I. D. (1970, 1971) *Deschooling Society.* London: Calder and Boyars.

People are schooled to confuse teaching with learning. Classic orthodox-challenging text: valuable for all teachers to work through.

Illich, I. D. (1973, 1974) *After Deschooling, What?* London: Writers' and Readers' Publishing Cooperative.

Schools reproduce society; skills should be shared. Short (22 page) anti-alienation pamphlet.

J

Jones, N. (ed.) (1989) *Special Educational Needs Review,* Vol. 2. Lewes: Falmer.

Specialist topics, including medical ones, and including gifted children.

Jones, N. and Frederickson, N. (eds) (1990) *Refocusing Educational Psychology.* London: Falmer.

Part of the 'education and alienation' series. Attempting to broaden the use of educational psychology in schools, from what the editors call a broadly humanistic and Gestalt perspective.

Carol Shillito-Clarke – Skills, Problem-solving and the Reflexive EP – provides a lovely, negative, description of the EP as

'the unknown and powerful "expert in difficult kids" who, some weeks following a request for help, descends from somewhere on high with a box of tricks, runs a test or two with the unfortunate child and then disappears back from whence he/she came to write a diagnostic report which, several weeks on again, will pronounce judgment on the child's academic future. EPs are perceived as being remote, humourless individuals who can only communicate with those who understand their jargon and suspect others of not doing their job as parent or teacher properly' (p. 56).

Norah Frederickson – Systems Approaches in EP Practice: A Re-evaluation – on what is a systems approach, and how can it be used (developed out of the theories of Checkland).

Neil Bolton – Educational Psychology and the Politics and Practice of Education – quotes Gaius Petronius, from 66 AD:

'We trained hard...but it seemed every time we were beginning to form up into teams we were reorganized. I was to learn later in life that we tend to meet any situation by reorganizing, and a wonderful method it can be for creating the illusion of progress while producing confusion, inefficiency, and demoralization' (p. 165).

K

Kelly, G. A. (1955) *The Psychology of Personal Constructs.* New York: Norton.

Key text of personal construct theory – i.e. ask about, look at, analyse a person's 'version' of themselves now, and work on what could be done with it.

Kimberley, K., Meek, M. and Miller, J. (eds) (1992) *New Readings: Contributions to an understanding of literacy.* London: A and C Black.

Working towards continuity and breadth, rather than taking sides in current arguments. Loads of lovely examples (from young children) of, e.g., oral storytelling, the music or rhythm of language, and so on. Articles are included on the philosophy and politics of literacy, the nature of interpretation, the role of the teacher, etc. An interesting article on old age and storytelling, too. Reading and learning to read are tied in to social practices, and are essentially changeable.

L

La Fontaine, J. (1991) *Bullying: The Child's View; An Analysis of Telephone Calls to ChildLine about bullying.* London: Calouste Gulbenkian Foundation.

As in the title, split according to categories, etc., including work on boarding schools. Useful. Excellent bibliography and resource list.

La Métais, J. (1985) *Homework Policy and Practice in Selected European Countries.* Brussels: Eurydice Central Unit.

A comparative study of homework practices. It is referred to in MacBeath and Turner (1990).

Laslett, R. and Smith, C. (1984) *Effective Classroom Management: A Teacher's Guide.* London: Croom Helm.

Excellent blow-by-blow guide: get them in (greeting, seating, starting), get them out (concluding, dismissing), get on with it (content, manner, organisation), get on with them (who's who, what's going on). The book contatins lovely case-studies, and plenty of guidance on self-evaluation. It is also totally bereft of jargon.

Lawton, D. and Dufour, B. (1973, 2nd edn. 1976) *The New Social Studies: A Handbook for Teachers in Primary, Secondary and Further Education.* London: Heinemann Educational.

A 'classic' text, especially good on secondary school subjects. Overtaken by the National Curriculum, but worth looking to for an historical overview – and history may well repeat itself. See also Dufour's book on NC Cross Curricular Themes, where some believe social sciences will re-assert themselves. The book covers the history of subjects, teaching methods and materials, possible topics or themes for use in the classroom (always useful), and evaluation.

Lennox, D. (1991) *See Me After School: Understanding and Helping Children with Emotional and Behavioural Difficulties.* London: David Fulton.

Good, broadly psychological approach, including stress (good stress chart on p 44), truancy, abuse, etc. Useful background and loads of snippets.

Lurie, A. (1990) *Don't Tell the Grown-Ups: Subversive Children's Literature.* London: Bloomsbury.

A lovely book, giving such insight into the complex world of children's understanding and imagination. An antidote to those views of children that simplify and clean up the whole business. Interesting, too, for those who want to understand, or teach, controversial issues.

M

McAlpine, A., Brown, S., McIntyre, D., and Hagger, H. (1988) *Student–Teachers Learning from Experienced Teachers.* Edinburgh: Scottish Council for Research in Education.

Joint work with Oxford University (presumably because of their mentor scheme). Good on simple methods of 'interviewing' teachers, to help them improve.

MacBeath, J. (1993) *A Place for Success: An Evaluation of Study Support in England Scotland and Northern Ireland.* London: The Prince's Trust.

Place-by-place analysis of study support (homework) centres. Great reading with perceptive analysis. (Also published as part of University of Strathclyde Quality in Education Centre for Research and Consultancy, 1993.)

MacBeath, J. and Turner, M. (1990) *Learning out of School: Report of Research Study Carried out at Jordanhill College.* Glasgow: Jordanhill College.

Probably the central text on homework and how it is (or could or should) be approached. Homework is defined as learning 'that is relevant to teachers' curricular objectives...which takes place outwith formal classroom teaching...which is primarily the responsibility of the learner himself/herself'. It is difficult or complex to prescribe or evaluate; schools have ambivalent attitudes to it because it can be great or can be merely ritualistic. Belgium bans homework below age of 10; Spain forbids it in all schools; Luxembourg sets maximum of 30 minutes in first year; etc. This study was based on 13 varied Scottish (primary and secondary) schools. Previous research suggested homework helped performance, for all pupils (as in Holmes and Croll, 1989), and was especially useful in early primary years. However, while 50% of pupils said that they enjoyed school, only 2% said they enjoyed homework – homework is (often) counterproductive and frustrating, demotivating pupils (as in Macfarlane, 1987). It is often badly set. A Dutch study found 94% of homework was given at the end of the lesson, half of the time after the bell had rung, and in 9% of cases during the ringing of the bell. MacBeath and Turner's study includes perceived purposes of homework (often left unstated); how people (pupils, teachers, parents) value homework; what the best (perceived) thing is about homework (it helps you learn); what the worst (perceived) thing is about homework (it takes too much time or stops you doing other things). Parental involvement is analysed, including critical comments. For example, with respect to copying out work lists, 'I am getting a mite scunnered wi' the words. I can see they have to do them but could they not make it a wee bit mair interesting wi' puzzles or crosswords. Dress it up, you know what I mean.' Problems are described of the transition from primary school (using simple, clear, maybe repetitive, tasks) to secondary school (using complex, unclear, varied, demanding, tasks). The amount of time spent on homework per evening in secondary schools: none, 9% (according to pupils) or 5% (according to parents); less than an hour, 41% or 43% respectively; 1–2 hours, 47% or 43%; 2–3 hours, 2% or 9%; over 3 hours, 0% or 1%. Homework is often solitary – 'The thing I like least about homework its that it is a lonely and tedious activity'. 'Homework has to be seen in the context of competing attractions such as television, but these need not be seen as the enemies of learning, and may be used constructively by teachers.' Primary parents help children with homework more than secondary parents (57% often or very often compared with 17%), generally because secondary parents feel they don't have the knowledge (though this varies with socio-economic group).

Note that 'A school's credibility in the community is often considerably affected by its approach to homework'. Monitoring homework is particularly valuable – perhaps in the lesson. Should failure to do it be punished? – 32% of secondary teachers thought it should never be punished. Note that with pupils with real problems 'Just laying off [i.e. not setting homework] doesn't necessarily help. It may be very important for a child struggling with her self-esteem to have homework like everyone else. It is possible to meet that personal and social need but at the same time make homework more manageable'. 'Finishing off' should not be too regularly the homework; self-contained/parallel homework can be set; spontaneous work is good; preparation (for the next lesson) is useful, though not so good for the insecure. Homework should be clearly related to classroom work; there should be a clear pattern; homework should be varied; homework should be manageable; homework should be challenging but not too difficult; homework should allow for individual initiative and creativity (good for motivation!); homework should promote self-confidence and understanding; there should be recognition of or reward for work done; there should be guidance and support. Parents need to be involved in developing policy, as well as in the practice of homework. Pupils should be involved in devising homework; homework should only be prescribed when it is purposeful and useful, and when it is put to use in class work or is followed by feedback from teacher and pupils. Adequate notice should be given. There is a need for inter-departmental co-ordination, discussing homework set, using seven criteria – purpose, level of difficulty, skills required, resources required, time required, range of activities involved, and opportunities for collaboration. Homework is never to be used as a punishment, and failure to do homework should never be punished by extra homework.

MacBeath, J., Thomson, B., Arrowsmith, J. and Forbes, D. (1992) *Using Ethos Indicators in Secondary School Self-Evaluation: Taking Account of the Views of Pupils, Parents, and Teachers: School Development Planning Support Materials*. *See* Scottish Office Education Department and HM Inspectors of Schools (1992).

Macdonald, I., Bhavnani, R., Khan, L. and John, G. (1989) *Murder in the Playground: The Report of the Macdonald Inquiry into Racism and Racial Violence in Manchester Schools*. London: Longsight Press.

A report, all the more shocking for its cool style, into a playground murder of an Asian boy by a white boy. The report is both into the incident and into more general issues, including the media coverage of the issue (the report was, astonishingly, distorted into an attack on anti-racist education), the local and national political response, the history of anti-racist education, and broader educational issues of empowerment, etc. Chapter 2 provides a chilling 10-page description of the stabbing and the events leading up to it, though I would caution against accepting some of the (selective and largely unwarranted by the evidence given) projection of feelings onto the boys (e.g. 'the bully was enjoying himself', p. 13). If any teacher fails to cringe at the description of muddle, inconsistency, and poor judgement, I'll eat my hat. Weep also over various letters and memos sent by various people (and think about your own letters), decisions made (the ambulance apparently wasn't called for until quite a while after the stabbing, white pupils were banned from the funeral of the murdered boy, bereavement counselling was provided for staff but not pupils, etc.). Various follow-up incidents (fights, etc.) are described, along with comments on how they were (and could have been) dealt with, and how (the report believes) the actions of the Head may have promoted racism, despite his commitment to the ideology of anti-racism. Racism amongst the teaching staff is chillingly reported (pp. 140-141), including comments on sending pupils 'back to Pakistan', and miscellaneous bullying. Staff bullying, according to the report, included allegedly blacking a colleague's face with shoe polish at a party because he was known to support anti-racism, or re-naming a deputy head 'Porky', wearing pig badges, and pinning pork scratching packets to his notice board, because he suggested turkey was more appropriate than pork for christmas dinner as it didn't exclude Muslims. Alleged comments by staff to pupils included 'you are like a cart load of monkeys; you are not fit to pray; in my country and my culture people respect women'. The book includes a lot, too, about general staffroom politics, including 'spies' and 'in' and 'out' groups. Other Manchester schools are studied, too, and the report concludes that the murder could have happened anywhere. Issues of class and of gender are well covered (unlike the Burnage anti-racist policy at that time), as are surveys into name-calling (p. 269 *et seq.*), etc.

(Burnage is reported to be a very different school now.)

McDonald, J. (1994) *Voices from Two Tongues: A Report on Aspects of the Experiences of Education of Bilingual School leavers in South*

Camden. London: Camden TVEI and Kingsway College.

> Background information, full accounts of, and analysis of, interviews with bilingual pupils or students. Also covered are the implications of the issues for FE. There are valuable insights, with significance for people studying progression as well as those studying bilingualism.

Macfarlane, E. (1987) Down with homework – bring back prep. *Times Education Supplement,* Nov. 1987 3725, p. 25.

> While 50% of pupils said that they enjoyed school, only 2% said they enjoyed homework. Homework is counterproductive and frustrating, demotivating pupils.

MacGilchrist, B. and Hall, V. (1993) *Using Management Development Materials: A Guide for Schools, Local Education Authorities and Other Support Agencies.* London: HMSO.

> A DFE booklet, on principles of (e.g.) INSET. It should be self-directed, flexible, school-determined, performance-enhancing, etc. Lots of examples, and a good set of references to practical materials and support agencies.

Maclure, S. (1988, 3rd edn., 1992) *Education Re-formed: A Guide to the Education Reform Act.* London: Hodder and Stoughton.

> Brief (180 pages) uncontroversial run-through, with a useful standard explanation of the context of the Act in post-war education.

Male, J. and Thompson, C. (1985) *The Educational Implications of Disability: A Guide for Teachers.* London: RADAR.

> Relatively simple technical guide, issue-by-issue (like D'Albert, 1989).

Mann, M. (ed.) (1983) *The Macmillan Student Encyclopedia of Sociology.* London: Macmillan.

> Excellent coverage of many issues dealt with by any researcher, not just sociologists. Each entry is quite detailed, some a page or two, and refers to further entries and books on the subject.

Marland, M. (1971) *Head of Department.* London: Heinemann Educational.

> Useful, sympathetic, non-dogmatic, guide – useful to members of departments as well as heads. The general principle is of the Head of Department supporting the members, doing the 'dirtiest' jobs, and representing the department to the outside world. This is only obvious if you don't know Heads of Department.

Marland, M. (1975, 1993) *The Craft of the Classroom: A Survival Guide.* Oxford: Heinemann Educational.

> Excellent general 'how to teach' book. Some people at first didn't like the idea of 'survival' as an aim – they thought you should aim higher. However, students and new teachers nearly always find the book useful, and it is good as a set of reminders: for

example, on a professional attitude of care (not too emotional or gushing), on clarity, on management of equipment and learning activities, on avoiding personal criticism, on apologising, on time-keeping (starting and finishing), on blackboard skills, on talking and questioning, on structuring lessons, etc.

Marland, M. (1989) *The Tutor and the Tutor Group: Developing Your Role as a Tutor.* London: Longman.

A very good, detailed, practical guide to all aspects of tutoring in a secondary school.

Miller, J. C. (1982) *Tutoring: the Guidance and Counselling Role of the Tutor in Vocational Preparation.* Hertford: NICEC.

A clear guide – as in the title – particularly useful for those working in post-16 education, but with much of use for teachers of older secondary pupils, too.

Moon, B., Murphy, P. and Raynor, J. (eds) (1989) *Policies for the Curriculum.* London: Hodder and Stoughton/Open University.

A set of heavyweight, authoritative, articles for the OU's MA. Useful and wide ranging – but needs to be unpicked.

Moon, B. and Shelton Mayes, A. (eds) (1994) *Teaching and Learning in the Secondary School.* London: Routledge/Open University.

An enormously action-packed set of articles put together for the OU's PGCE, but it will no doubt be used by many others. Some articles are well-known heavyweights, others are (or were) obscure. All the obvious topics are covered. A very modern feel to it that will, I hope, be retained over the years.

Murphy, P. and Moon, B. (eds) (1989) *Developments in Learning and Assessment.* London: Hodder and Stoughton/Open University.

A set of heavyweight, authoritative, articles for the OU's MA. Useful and wide ranging.

N

National Association for Remedial Education In-Service Training Sub-Committee (Cripps, C. *et al.*) (1990) *Planning Your School-Based Inset: A Framework for Meeting Special Educational Needs.* NARE Publications.

'A course should comprise: "something old, something new, something to talk about and something to do".'

National Commission on Education (1993) *Briefings for the Paul Hamlyn Foundation National Commission on Education.* London: Heinemann.

Written for the academic as well as general reader. More pithy, exciting, even controversial, than its tamed companion (*Learning to Succeed*), with each chapter starting with an extremely useful summary. Measuring added value in schools; managing teachers; participation of 16–18 year-olds in education and training; teacher shortages; breaking out of the low-skill equilibrium; higher education (by Halsey); selection for

secondary schooling (and comprehensives) (by Geoffrey Walford); early childhood
education; Initial teacher education; standards in literacy and numeracy; General
Teaching Council; class size; parental choice; SEN – the next 25 years (by Klaus Wedell);
careers; raising standards in deprived urban areas (by Michael Barber); finance for
students in HE; local democracy for the learning society; moral and spiritual education;
educational technology ('the classroom of 2015'). The references alone would be useful.
The overall philosophy is social democratic in its broadest and vaguest sense.

National Commission on Education (1993) *Learning to Succeed: Report of the Paul Hamlyn Foundation National Commission on Education.* London: Heinemann.

Written for the general reader (unlike their Briefings, which is used more by
academics). On education and training, with a pragmatic yet 'visionary' (in its
management-speak version) programme for development. Their historical accounts
seem sound, their statistics are detailed (for example, the average KS1 teachers had 22
minutes per week non-contact time, while 80% of secondary teachers had over 3 hours
– p. 224), their conclusions are sensible, and their style (perhaps of chair Lord Walton)
is efficient if rather committee-ish. Post-National Curriculum but pre-Dearing: 'The
more time that teachers can spend on teaching, and pupils on learning, the better'
(p. 197). Such unexceptionable conclusions are tied up with more interesting
recommendations about administration, etc. There is plenty on student teachers, pay,
nursery education, adult education, etc., as well as the obvious 'quality' (or
'effectiveness') topics. The book recommends setting up Education and Training
Boards, to take over some LEA and some DFE responsibilities, with an 'arms length'
style. There must be more national investment in education and training. Overall, a
good report, that could be taken-up, wholesale, by any major political party. I guess that
it will become one of the defining texts of the educational culture of the 1990s.

National Council for Educational Technology (1990) *Developing Partnerships between Librarians and Teachers in Flexible Learning.* Coventry: NCET.

A well-produced pack, more a training manual than just a 'position paper', that goes
well beyond the rather narrow title. It should stimulate good discussion amongst all
manner of teachers and their non-teaching colleagues.

National Oracy Project (1991) *Assessment Through Talk in Key Stages 3 and 4.* Occasional Papers in Oracy No. 4; London: National Oracy Project.

Case studies, as in the title. Useful for combating cynicism, and for getting simple
ideas. (*See also* Norman, 1992, and Open University, 1991.)

National Union of Teachers (1983) *Combating Racism in Schools.* London: NUT.

Good, punchy, brief (19 pages) of basic background and examples of policies. Useful
for raising issues, though, of course, too short to deal with them all.

NCC (National Curriculum Council) (1991) *Teaching Talking and*

Learning in Key Stage Three: A Booklet for Teachers Based on the Work of The National Oracy Project. York: NCC and National Oracy Project.

Loads of different techniques, on using talk and much much more. There is plenty on group work, gender, bilingualism, and everything else. A nice simple quotation from Douglas Barnes, too: 'The best teachers are those who choose deliberately and inventively amongst a repertoire of learning activities, or who can judge when the pupils themselves can choose the strategies most likely to advance their learning'.

Neame, R. (director); Allen, J. P. (writer); Spark, M. (author of novel) (1969) *The Prime of Miss Jean Brodie.* TCF.

Film of the book – both are good, especially at showing the problems that can arise even from being an enthusiastic teacher. The problems seem to come from the heroine's attitude to her pupils as extensions of her own personality, and from the art teacher's breaking with professionalism.

Newton, C. and Tarrant T. (1992) *Managing Change in Schools: A Practical Handbook.* London: Routledge.

A book by educational psychologists, mostly centred on research done in primary, rather than secondary, schools – linking change at individual, family, school, LEA, etc., level:

'Children learn – so can schools'.

'The initial task is not to converge on a definition of a problem to solve, but to build up the richest possible picture of the situation in question, drawing on the disparate perceptions of those involved.'

'Examine the school rituals to reflect and celebrate policy and practice. Rituals need to be rewarding; enjoyment needs to be part of the range of rituals' (p. 134).

'Unhappy, stressed workaholics are not good role models for young people and are unlikely to retain the good humour and positive attitudes required. There is no merit in any occupation in allowing it to damage you or others. In the last resort teaching is an occupation to be followed professionally. This does not mean that we are advocating a very limited view of work demands. Hard work can be and usually is good for people. One of the best ways to stop worrying about tasks that have to be done is to do them. The problems come when the quality of work is poor and the stress symptoms take over' (pp. 194–195).

Norman, K. (ed.), (1992) *Thinking Voices: The Work of the National Oracy Project.* London: Hodder and Stoughton.

A series of brief, useful, articles on talk in the classroom – including practical and theoretical issues. Interesting on, for example, 'standard English' (by Tony Edwards), on 'scaffolding' as a way of looking at teaching (by Janet Maybin, Neil Mercer and Barry Stierer), and on gender (by Hilary Kemeny). (*See also* National Oracy Project, 1991; and Open University, 1991.)

Northern Ireland Council for Educational Development (1989) *A School Homework Policy: Primary Guidelines Support Paper.* Belfast: NICED.

Professional opinion is divided on how useful homework is – with the Department of Education for Northern Ireland saying (1981/15) 'It remains the opinion of the Department that formal homework is not essential for pupils in primary schools and preparatory departments'.

O

Office for Standards in Education (1993) *Framework for the Inspection of Schools.* London: OFSTED.

Useful and well-written 40-page guide to inspection, written, I would imagine, for schools. OFSTED has become a much-feared institution – perhaps just because it is new. If this booklet is anything to go by, then, eventually, there should be little to fear, unless your school is unwilling to demonstrate how good it is in the way OFSTED expect. Certainly, it is the way of demonstrating good qualities (and the fact that schools have often worked to different, albeit equally valid, criteria in the past), rather than those qualities themselves, that seems to scare schools. Each section of this framework includes evaluation criteria, what evidence needs to be included, and what will be said in the report. Although paperwork (e.g. departmental policies) is clearly important, it seems clear that good practice, matching the paperwork, is also – reasonably enough – required. This document is useful, and is interesting in its own right (particularly for people doing research into schools) as it addresses problems such as the validity of quantitative and qualitative data.

Open University (1991) *Talk and Learning 5–16: An In-Service Pack on Oracy for Teachers.* Milton Keynes: Open University.

A self-explanatory title. (*See also* National Oracy Project, 1991, and Norman, 1992.)

Oswin, M. (1991) *Am I Allowed to Cry?: A Study of Bereavement amongst People who have Learning Difficulties.* London: Souvenir Press.

A superb, concise (159 page), lesson in respect and sensitivity, very applicable to all children (and adults). It ends with 73 recommendations and suggestions. A model of its kind.

P

Peter, M. (ed.) (1992) *Differentiation: Ways Forward;.* Stafford: National Association for Special Educational Needs. (Reprinted from the *British Journal of Special Education,* 1992, **19, (1)**.)

I regard this as the best book on differentiation, especially the key article by Penelope Weston (A Decade for Differentiation – with 'decade' meaning a series of 10). Weston points out the difference between perspectives of differentiation between groups and differentiation between individuals (as in Stradling and Saunders, 1991). The first perspective reflects uncertainty over whether the same basic goals of education should apply to all pupils. The second perspective implies diversity – i.e. learners differ. Differentiation is in this way seen as multi-dimensional (not just, for example, high, middle and low ability):

● differentiation applies to individuals (teachers can't create homogeneous groups – but they needn't have wholly individualised work schemes, as team work is vital);

● differentiation applies to all learners (it is not just a euphemism for helping low attainers!);

● differentiation is diagnostic (i.e. there is a need to link it with systems of assessment and records of achievement);

● differentiation challenges expectations;

● differentiation challenges classroom relationships (so the teacher can't just 'teach to the middle', and pupils will probably take more responsibility);

● differentiation is an integral aspect of effective learning (it must include flexible learning, and must be part of departmental curriculum planning).

Differentiation is relevant for all teachers (not just support teachers!), and it requires a long-term, whole-school strategy.

Another useful article is that by Ann Lewis (From Planning to Practice) – on practical methods of differentiation. This covers differentiation by content, interests, pace, level, access, response or outcome, sequence, structure, teacher time, teaching style, and grouping. Lewis goes on to ask which of these are most effective. Streaming, she says, tends to lower the self-esteem of children in lower streams. Within mixed-ability classes, similar ability grouping is effective for specific 'academic' tasks, but mixed ability groups are preferable for open-ended or creative tasks. Collaborative (contrasted with parallel or competitive) types of group are associated with effective problem-solving for children at certain stages of acquiring understanding. Children with difficulties in learning benefit from structured sequencing and subdividing.

An article by Michael Hart includes the types of differentiation used at a secondary school – individualised schemes (as for Maths); open-ended tasks; circus arrangements; resources at different levels being available to all pupils in the class (and they select); groupwork; tasks where the final product is gradually drafted, with each pupil working to improve those aspects of the piece that are particularly relevant to them; use of a variety of media, not just written texts.

The book as a whole also has plenty of other book references and reviews.

Plowden Report – *see* Central Advisory Council for Education.

R

Redmond, P. (devised the series) and Hush, S. (the producer) (1980–) *Grange Hill.* London: BBC.

The best child's-eye view of comprehensive school life. Unusual in using camera angles that make the programmes literally at the level of children. All kinds of key issues covered, both in the classroom, in the community, and in the lives of the pupils. Perhaps in more recent series, the personal lives of the pupils have taken over from broader educational issues. Good training for teachers; I try to base my teaching technique on the nice Scottish CDT teacher, incidentally.

Richardson, R. (1990) *Daring to be a Teacher: Essays, Stories and Memoranda*. Stoke-on-Trent: Trentham.

Varied short pieces on the morality of education: racism, attitudes of teachers, policies, etc. An insider's educational philosophy, put forward in fragments of prose, poetry, and epigrams.

Roberts, R. (1987) *A Ragged Schooling*. Manchester: Manchester University Press.

Working-class Salford autobiography before World War One. Good, if a little rosy, accounts of school and night classes, from the perspective of someone who might have been expected to have been a failure.

Roberts, W. (1989) *Leadership Secrets of Attila the Hun*. London: Bantam Books.

Rather bizarre, compulsive, reconstruction of Attila's probable techniques, endlessly applicable – not least to teachers both in the classroom and the staffroom. Surprisingly similar to Laslett and to Marland. Only examples can give a flavour:

'Discipline should be expected only at those levels of order and conformity that serve the good of the tribe or nation. Demanding more than is required is an abuse of power and will give rise to rebellion within the tribe.'

'Never allow your Huns too many idle moments. These give rise to the beginnings of discontent'.

'Never cast blame for failure upon the guiltless'.

'Never threaten the security or esteem of another Hun unless you are prepared to deal with the consequences.'

'Be principled, not inflexible.'

'Do not expect everyone to agree with you – even if you are king.'

'It takes less courage to criticize the decisions of others than to stand by your own.'

'Chieftains who ask the wrong questions always hear the wrong answers.'

'A chieftain should always rise above pettiness and cause his Huns to do the same.'

Rutter, M., Maughan, B., Mortimore, P. and Ouston, J. (1979) *Fifteen Thousand Hours: Secondary Schools and their Effect on Children*. London: Open Books.

Probably the all-time favourite sociology book for headteachers. Basically a statistical analysis of measurable school variables (attendance, punctuality, buildings, discipline systems, exam results, pupil crime, etc.) across a dozen schools. The authors found that there was a correlation between qualities such as positive rewards and teacher punctuality, and outcomes such as low truancy rates, good behaviour, and good exam results. The conclusion: schools can make a difference, whatever the school buildings are like, especially if the teachers are well prepared. Hence the popularity with headteachers. The authors have been unreasonably accused of sociological naïvety, and of over-playing the significance of statistics: both in presenting correlations as causes, and in presenting the differences between schools as more significant than the similarities. However, the book itself does tackle these questions.

On the single topic of homework, as on many other topics, there is plenty of information. 'Academically successful schools tended to have an emphasis on examinations and on homework' (p. 11). There is a significant correlation between homework seen in first year classes and behaviour (not attendance, academic, or delinquency outcomes). And so on. Statistics on time spent on homework 'do not show how and why homework is associated with better outcomes. But it may well be that in addition to its practical value in providing opportunities for the consolidation of the learning of work introduced in school time, homework may also be of symbolic importance in emphasising the school's concern for academic progress, and its expectation that pupils have the ability and self-discipline needed to work without direct supervision.' There was a significant correlation (of 0.52) between checking (generally informally by senior colleagues) on whether teachers set homework, and academic outcomes.

S

Salmon, P. (1988) *Psychology for Teachers: An alternative approach.* London: Hutchinson Education.

The alternative being to mechanistic psychology. Salmon's approach is to apply Kelly's personal construct theory, that gave 'central importance...to the idea that each of us creates our own reality, that we can know the whole world we live in only through the personal interpretations, or constructions, that we make of it' (p. 11). Education is not simply a search for understanding, it is a transformation of character – as in the story of Adam and Eve. This is equally important to understanding teachers as it is to understanding pupils. Education is personal. A thoroughly sensitive book that, in line with the perspective it espouses, acknowledges and respects the views of those actually involved in teaching.

Salzberger-Wittenberg, I., Henry, G. and Osborne, E. (1983) *The Emotional Experience of Learning and Teaching.* London: Routledge and Kegan Paul.

Powerful, useful, and surprising book, that should be read at different stages of a career – to provide different insights. Based on the (Freudian/Kleinian) work of the Tavistock Clinic, but readily applicable to schools. The book looks at teaching and learning in terms of beginnings (hopes and fears), relationships (idealised, denigratory, helpful), and endings (loss, breaking up, etc.). It is quite heavy going, but is worth persevering with.

Sandblom, P. (1982) *Creativity and Disease: How Illness Affects Literature, Art and Music.* New York: Marion Boyars.

A peculiar book, that loosely ties the illness of certain artists to their works, whilst avoiding any grand theories on the issues.

Scoffham, S. (1980) *Using the School's Surroundings: A Guide to Local Studies in Urban Schools.* London: Ward Lock.

Practical, case-study-based, guide, based on work mainly done in South West London primary schools. Particularly good on pre-planning (what if it rains? etc.) and follow-up or display. Useful for secondary teachers, too.

Scottish Office Education Department and HM Inspectors of Schools (1992) *Using Ethos Indicators in Secondary School Self-Evaluation: Taking Account of the Views of Pupils, Parents, and Teachers: School Development Planning Support Materials.* Edinburgh: Scottish Office Education Department.

This is the book of the project directed by John MacBeath and Bill Thomson, with Judith Arrowsmith and David Forbes. (There is an accompanying book available on the primary school project.) A lovely, lovely, book, despite its unspeakable title and amateur binding of glue and insulating tape. It is the best book I've seen on how to do school research – at any level (A level, PGCE, PhD, INSET, etc.). White pages are 'how to do it' pages; yellow pages are 'the experiences of schools' pages (i.e. examples). The 'how to' sections include how to collect information (e.g. offering raffle tickets for a bottle of whisky to each teacher completing a questionnaire, to get a 100% response rate); how to collate and process the data; how to analyse and interpret the responses; how to select items for analysis. There is an account of the 12 ethos indicators used: pupil morale (i.e. 'The degree to which pupils enjoy school and find it a safe and satisfying place to be'), teacher morale, teachers' job satisfaction, the physical environment, the learning context, teacher–pupil relationships, equality and justice, extra-curricular activities, school leadership, discipline, information to parents, parent-teacher consultation. The book gives great, clear, descriptions, and offers examples of questionnaire items for each indicator.

Searle, C. (compiler) (1975) *Classrooms of Resistance.* London: Writers' and Readers' Publishing Cooperative.

Compiled by a teacher famous (at the time) for being sacked and (on protests from pupils and teachers) reinstated as a teacher in East London. Searle's collection is of passionately political poetry, prose and plays, written by his pupils. Interesting in all sorts of ways.

Shaw, R. (1987) *Children of Imprisoned Fathers.* London: Hodder and Stoughton.

Written primarily for probation officers, social workers and prison staff, with nothing specifically on schooling. Useful, though, as a way of looking at hidden victims, and at stigma. The book should at least sensitise teachers to the issues.

Simmons, J. (ed.) (1980) *The Education Dilemma: Policy Issues for Developing Countries in the 1980s.* Oxford: Pergamon.

Interesting but heavyweight accounts of key issues, with an economic bias – understandable, given the pedigree. Some issues (such as 'can education solve the unemployment problem?') are just as relevant to 'developed' countries. It is particularly interesting to see how the UK government in the 1980s used some of the approaches used earlier by 'developing' countries, for example on (un)employment and on centralisation and political control of the education system.

Simon, B. (1991) *Education and the Social Order, 1940–1990.* London: Lawrence and Wishart.

Spackman, F. (1991) *Teachers' Professional Responsibilities.* London: David Fulton and The Roehampton Institute.

Brief (102 page) practical guide to being a teacher (other than the teaching), covering interviews/professional development, health and safety, unions (including a guide to their services), relationships with staff, parents and pupils, etc. All things all teachers need to know, but won't know they need to know until it's already too late. Sensible advice in a legal framework.

Spender, D. (1982) *Invisible Women: The Schooling Scandal.* London: Writers' and Readers' Collective.

Classic text on how girls are ignored in school. A must-read for anyone who thinks there isn't a problem.

Stradling, R. and Saunders, L., with Weston, P. (1991) *Differentiation in Action: a Whole School Approach for Raising Attainment.* Slough: NFER.

A nice practical book, clearly set out.

Strauss, A. L. and Corbin, J. (1990) *Basics of Qualitative Research: Grounded Theory Procedures and Techniques.* London: Sage.

Fourth of the series (Glaser and Strauss, 1967, Glaser, 1978, *Strauss Qualitative Analysis for Social Scientists*, 1987). This book the most detailed for *learning* qualitative analysis. Qualitative research refers (p. 18) to 'a nonmathematical analytical procedure that results in findings derived from data gathered by a variety of means.'

Swann, W. (ed.) (1981) *The Practice of Special Education.* Oxford: Blackwell and the Open University Press.

Open University reader on (mostly physical) special needs. Articles on history are included, as well as on (then) current provision. Now outdated, but with some useful snippets.

T

Tattum, D. and Herbert, G. (1990) *Bullying: A Positive Response.* Cardiff: South Glamorgan Institute of Higher Education.

Thomas, D. (1978) *The Social Psychology of Childhood Disability.* London: Methuen.

An interesting book on public attitudes. It talks of people's 'revulsion to compassion'.

Tingle, M (1990) *The Motor Impaired Child.* Windsor. NFER-Nelson.

An eminently practical account, which analyses impairment and gives a guide to practice. Very reliable.

Tomlinson, S. (1982) *A Sociology of Special Education*. London: Routledge and Kegan Paul.

A fairly standard historical approach, including Warnock, but written a bit early to take account of the implications of the 1981 Act.

Topping, K. (1988) *The Peer Tutoring Handbook: Promoting Co-operative Learning*. London: Croom Helm.

A practical guide for using (and monitoring, assessing, etc.) peer tutoring in schools.

Topping, K. J. (1986) *Parents as Educators: Training Parents to Teach Their Children*. London: Croom Helm.

The book, by an Educational Psychologist, deals, in particular, with 'problem' issues – SEN, ethnicity, etc.

Tough, J. (1976) *Listening to Children Talking*. London: Ward Lock.

Extremely detailed study of language used by pupils aged 3 to 7, packed with examples of conversations and exercises and projects, including pictures that can be used to stimulate (and assess) children's talking. *See also* Tough, J. (1979) *Talk for Teaching and Learning*. London: Ward Lock (for pupils aged 7 to 13), and Tough, J. (1981) *A Place for Talk: The Role of Talk in the Education of Children with Moderate Learning Difficulties;* London: Ward Lock (for pupils with MLD).

TVEI (1988) *TVEI Developments 5: Profiles and Records of Achievement*. Sheffield: MSC.

A set of brief articles, mostly describing good practice in profiling and ROA (records of achievement).

TVEI (1989) *TVEI Developments 10: Flexible Learning*. Sheffield: Training Agency.

A set of brief articles, mostly describing good practice in flexible learning – including the use of (information) technology, libraries, and resource-based learning. It is good to get an overview of student-centred learning in practice.

'By giving the student increasing responsibility for his or her own learning within a framework of support, teachers will find that, as well as learning the discrete school subjects, students will also develop a range of personal, social, information handling and learning-to-learn skills which considerably enhance personal effectiveness and help contribute to equalise and optimise opportunities for them' (Trayers).

U

University of Strathclyde Quality in Education Centre for Research and Consultancy, in association with the Strathclyde Regional Council Department of Education (1993) *Study Support Resources Pack;* London: The Prince's Trust.

Videos and study booklet on how to promote, set up and run a study support centre. An expensive pack, worth every penny. (It incorporates MacBeath, 1993.)

V

Varma, V. (ed.) (1992) *The Secret Life of Vulnerable Children.* London: Routledge.

Various psychiatric and psychotherapeutic views of, for example, depressed, neurotic, autistic, abused, hyperactive, etc., children.

W

Walford, G. (ed.) (1992) *Doing Educational Research.* London: Routledge.

Personal accounts by many leading education researchers (Stephen J. Ball, Barbara Tizard, Peter Mortimore, and so on) of the process of research. Useful insight into the practical issues facing real researchers but rarely covered in the books produced by that research or in the books about research methods. Problems of access to schools, and to staff and pupils in schools, are well covered, for example, in Walford's own article on research in a CTC.

Warnock Report – *see* Committee of Enquiry into the Education of Handicapped Children and Young People.

Waterhouse, P. (1988) *Supported Self-Study: An Introduction for Teachers.* London: Council for Educational Technology.

Webster, A. and Ellwood, J. (1985) *The Hearing-Impaired Child in the Ordinary School.* London: Croom Helm.

Good, detailed account, including a lot of technical information. Very useful 'warning signs' section at the end of the book – useful, particularly, as hearing impairment is often not diagnosed, and, undiagnosed, is one of the most common causes of apparent underachievement and misbehaviour.

Wehlage, *et al.* (1989) *Reducing the Risk: Schools as Communities of Support.* London: Falmer.

A deep, and always sympathetic, book on American schools dealing with 'drop outs'.

Frank Lloyd Wright: 'From the ground up makes good sense for building. Beware of from the top down.'

'Our findings suggest that careful attention by adults to social relations produces school membership for at-risk students, and that this membership depends upon specific commitments and practices by adults. School membership becomes a fundamental concept in the theory explaining how schools can prevent students from dropping out.'

'School as a community of support is a broad concept in which school membership and educational engagement are central. School membership is concerned with a sense of belonging and social bonding to the school and its members. Educational engagement is defined as involvement in school activities but especially traditional classroom and academic work.'

Weihs, T. J. (1971) *Children in Need of Special Care.* London: Souvenir Press.

The Steiner approach is clearly described here. The account is based on what it is like to be a (handicapped) child, understood through empathy, love, intuition or aesthetic appreciation, as much as through science. The book avoids jargon, and encourages optimism, not least in recommending the creation of adult communities like Steiner schools. It should be used by teachers (of all children) as a model of giving value to individuals, and avoiding rigid categorisation.

Wellington, J. J. (ed) (1986) *Controversial Issues in the Curriculum.* Oxford: Basil Blackwell.

There are varied, always interesting, articles on the theory and practice of teaching controversial issues. Issues covered include global education, gender, multicultural teaching, vocationalism, the 'facts of life', religion, peace studies, and nuclear issues.

Jean Rudduck (A strategy for handling controversial issues in the secondary school): 'The critical thinking that fosters scepticism and independence of mind is too much absent from the curriculum of the comprehensive school' (p. 6). These qualities are sometimes seen as alternatives to, for example, exam success. Rudduck's approach (from a Humanities Project) is based on five premises:

'1 that controversial issues should be handled in the classroom with adolescents; 2 that teachers should not use their authority as a platform for promoting their own views; 3 that the mode of inquiry in controversial areas should have discussion rather than instruction as its core; 4 that the discussion should protect divergence of view among participants and not force a consensus (unless of course group action necessitated a common perspective and plan); 5 that the teacher as chairperson of the discussion should have responsibility for ensuring proper exploration of the issue, using evidence as appropriate, and for quality of understanding' (p. 8).

The article includes some of the practical difficulties inherent in this sort of approach.

Welsh Consumer Council (1985) *WCC's response to 'Homework' – A Consultation Paper from the Department of Education and Science.* Cardiff: WCC.

A report that stresses the need for partnership between parents and the providers of the educational service. Homework, it says, is the third most cited area of concern of parents about their children's education.

Westmacott, E. V. S. and Cameron, R. J. (1981) *Behaviour Can Change.* Basingstoke: Macmillan Education.

A guide to the practice of behaviour modification. The central principles are to reinforce (but not too much) good behaviour, and to unlearn bad behaviour. It is a simple well-structured approach, even if it misses out the subtlety of the meaning and significance of ('bad') behaviour. Perhaps the simplicity of the approach is its best point. A star chart is easier to initiate than, for example, the promotion of anti-racism throughout society, or intensive family psychotherapy for every child behaving 'badly'.

Whitty, G. (1990) The Politics of the 1988 Education Reform Act, in Dunleavy, P., Gamble, A. and Peele, G. (eds) *Developments in British Politics 3*. Basingstoke: Macmillan Education.

Clear brief (12 page) account of the immediate background to, and opposition to, the 1988 Act. It is a fairly standard, critical, interpretation of the Act's market orientation, providing a useful basis for further work.

Whyte, J., Deem, R., Kant, L. and Cruikshank, M. (eds) (1985) *Girl Friendly Schooling*. London: Methuen.

A clear and very detailed analysis of sex bias, ways of making schooling more girl friendly, and possible future developments. Much good work is described on policies, on myths about women teachers as well as about girls, and possible INSET focuses.

Widlake, P. (ed.) (1989) *Special Children Handbook: Meeting Special Needs Within the Mainstream School*. London: Hutchinson.

Many very practical articles, on issues including difficult children; children with reading and language difficulties; children with severe disabilities; information technology, maths, science, art and music education and special needs; and policies on special needs, with lots of attention given to the role of parents.

Willis, P. (1977) *Learning to Labour: How Working Class Kids Get Working Class Jobs*. Farnborough, Hants: Saxon House.

A famous book on the cause and significance of subcultures within schools, based on a broadly Marxist economic foundation. The class structure beyond the school helps to create the hidden curriculum within the school, but pupils themselves help create their own futures. The book looks mostly at male anti-school subcultures, with rebellion seen as a response to judgements made about likely future employment. There are lively, funny, convincing, reports of interviews.

Wragg, E. C. (1981) *Class Management and Control*. Basingstoke: Macmillan Education.

A well-liked, practical, text.

Index

QUALITY IN SECONDARY SCHOOLS AND COLLEGES SERIES

Series Editor, Clyde Chitty

This new series publishes on a wide range of topics related to succesful education for the 11–19 age group. It reflects the growing interest in whole-school curriculum planning, together with the effective teaching of individual subjects and themes. There will also be books devoted to management and administration, examinations and assessment, pastoral care strategies, relationships with parents and governors and the implications for schools of changes in teacher education.

Early titles include:

Active History in Key Stages 3 and 4
Alan Farmer and Peter Knight
1–85346–305–1

English and Ability
Edited by Andrew Goodwyn
1–85346–299–3

English and the OFSTED Experience
Bob Bibby and Barrie Wade
1–85346–357–4

English as a Creative Art: Literary Concepts Linked to Creative Writing
Linden Peach and Angela Burton
1–85346–368-X

Geography 11–16: Rekindling Good Practice
Bill Marsden
1–85346–296–9

Heeding Heads: Secondary Heads and Educational Commentators in Dialogue
Edited by David Hustler, Tim Brighouse and Jean Rudduck
1–85346–358–2

The Literate Imagination: Renewing the Secondary English Curriculum
Bernard T. Harrison
1–85346–300–0

Making Sense of English: the National Curriculum
Roger Knight
1–85346–374–4

Managing the Learning of History
Richard Brown
1–85346–345–0

Moral Education through English 11–16
Ros McCulloch and Margaret Mathieson
1–85346–276–4

Partnership in Secondary Initial Teacher Education
Edited by Anne Williams
1–85346–361–2